General Patton's
SECRET
MISSIONS

*Little Known Facts
About Intriguing
Experiences Of Old
Blood And Guts*

RICHARD J. STILLMAN, Ph.D.
Colonel, U.S. Army (Ret.)

Visit our Website: www.rjstillman.com for a review of our available publications and services.

Published by:
R.J. Stillman Company
2311 Oriole Street
New Orleans, LA 70122
Phone (504) 288-8112
Fax (504) 286-7630

Library of Congress Control Number: 200545121

ISBN: 0-9650906-5-5

Printed in the United States of America

This book is printed on acid-free paper

10 9 8 7 6 5 4 3 2 1

Other Publications and Services Available

From the R.J. Stillman Company

Books:
- *General Patton's Timeless Leadership Principles: Your Practical Guide for a Successful Career and Life*
- *General Patton's Best Friend: The Story of General George S. Patton, Jr. and his Beloved Dog, Willie*

Charts:
- *Dow Jones Industrial Average: 1896-Present*
- *Life Span of General George S. Patton, Jr.: 1885-1945*
- *Super Bowls & Dow Industrials: 1967-1993*

Videos:
- *General Patton's Timeless Leadership Principles*
- *The Life & Times of General George S. Patton, Jr.*

Services:
- Patton Photos
- Lectures
- Seminars

CONTENTS

Appendices

FIGURES

Part Five   **Page**

ACKNOWLEDGEMENTS

A number of individuals deserve my heartfelt thank you for providing helpful assistance in making this book a reality.

In Section One I provide little known facts in regard to General Patton's key role in Operation Fortitude. A major contributor was the National D-Day Museum (New Orleans, Louisiana) and members of its staff. I would like to especially recognize the late Stephen E. Ambrose, my good friend and colleague, Gordon H. Mueller, President of the D-Day Museum, and Louise Fletcher, Manager of the eminently successful Museum Gift Shop.

Dr. Olof Lundberg (Chairman of the Management Department, University of New

Orleans) and his son also gave me valuable data on the Spear of Longinus.

Without the invaluable, professional work, careful review, and administrative skills of Mary E. Draughn, this book would have been long delayed.

General Patton, my old boss, deserves a nod of appreciation. Without his exciting life, to include intrepid experiences, the book would not have been possible.

DEDICATION

To my old boss

General George Smith Patton, Jr.

as well as all people

who have made

Operation Fortitude so successful

and my friends who provided

information on:

Huntington; Luxembourg

Cemetery; Conversation with

God; Spear of Longinus

PREFACE

These five stories are significant in highlighting the mystic of General Patton. The first three are factual experiences that emphasize his imaginative approach to being a successful leader. It further points up Patton's immense popularity based on visits to his gravesite. The first three are factual.

Part One indicates his ability to require the Germans to maintain 18 Divisions and supporting troops in the Pas de Calais region of France.

The second part highlights Old Blood and Guts recognition of history. He saw the significance of the Nuremberg Laws and the rare Edition of *Mein Kampf.*

The final factual segment indicates Patton's continual hold on world history. People come from all walks of life, from the highest representatives of countries to ordinary citizens. I was privileged to make three visits to the Luxembourg Cemetery with the latest being in 1998. At the head of the Cemetery is Patton's burial spot and his majestic presence could be felt by all of his former Staff members who were in attendance.

The final two stories point up the imagination powers of writers to expand on reality. The first tale is entitled "Conversation with God". It makes good reading; however, Patton never had this session with the Lord. He even fooled the Ambassador to Luxembourg who donated a plaque, presenting the Conversation with God. It appears at the entrance to our old Headquarters in Luxembourg City.

The second tale pertains to the belief that Patton acquired the Spear of Longinus. This was the

Lance that pierced the body of Jesus and was thrust into him by a soldier named Longinus. There is no shred of evidence indicating that Patton had any interest in the Spear. It currently resides in a museum in Austria.

In summary these five stories about my old boss captured my attention as the best examples of his immense popularity. He had great stage presence when we served with him and his appeal continues even stronger today.

Who was George Smith Patton, Jr.? I realize that at this writing (Fall 2004) that most readers were not alive when General Patton died in 1945. Therefore I would like to provide a brief background on the man.

He was born on November 11, 1885 and graduated from the United States Military Academy at West Point, New York in 1909. A year later he married Beatrice Banning Ayer, a socialite from Boston. The couple had three children, Beatrice, Ellen and George.

His first claim to fame was in the Punitive Expedition (1916-17) as an aide to General Pershing. He killed several banditos and his feat appeared in the New York Times. His service with General Pershing continued in World War I when Pershing commanded the American Expeditionary Force in Europe. His selection was due in some measure to a friendship that developed between the General and Patton's sister.

Between 1917 – 1918, Patton advanced in rank from Lieutenant to Colonel. He commanded a Tank Brigade and was awarded the Distinguished Service Cross (DSC).

Prior to World War II, he held the normal peacetime assignments. His expertise with armor enabled him to receive promotions from Colonel to four star General (1940-45). He died in Germany as the result of an automobile accident on December 21, 1945.

Part One

WHY OPERATION FORTITUDE WAS VITAL TO D-DAY'S SUCCESS

This book is divided into five parts. The initial section discusses General Patton's significant role in the success of Operation Fortitude during the European campaigns in World War II. I observed General Patton on a daily basis from March 1944 to October 1945. Based on my experiences and long time research, I point out the General's leadership as head of a fictitious Army Group.

INTRODUCTION

"Remember, I'm not here." Those were the words that General George Smith Patton, Jr. greeted us with on our arrival in England as new members of our Third Army Staff. This event took place early in March 1944. It was my privilege to serve on Patton's staff for nineteen months.

I would like to recount Patton's role in the secret mission code-named: Operation Fortitude. But first, let me provide background leading up to Fortitude.

I was commissioned a Regular Army second lieutenant of infantry in 1942. After graduating from the University of Southern California in 1938, I attended Harvard University for graduate study. A year later I went on active duty. I was initially a platoon leader in the Second Infantry and my unit went on maneuvers in Louisiana during the summer of 1940. That assignment gave me my first glimpse of George Smith Patton, Jr. He was an umpire for the largest United States military was games up to that time. Colonel Patton gave an impressive analysis at the end of the maneuvers with ample profanity to drive home his message.

General Patton came back to the Louisiana Maneuvers the next year as Commander of the Second Armored Division and really showed our senior military leaders how armor could be utilized in the best way in any combat situation.

After a year in the field, I was assigned to the War Department General Staff in Washington, D.C. General George C. Marshall was the Army Chief of

Staff. We were located in a temporary building on Constitution Avenue. Next door was another temporary building occupied by the Navy. The Chief of Naval Operations and his staff were located there. The two buildings were called temporary because they were built during World War I and were to be town down after the war. My Washington, D.C. duty was a great experience for me as a young lieutenant. It gave me the opportunity to observe and meet some of the present and future leaders of the Armed Forces.

I stayed in Washington, D.C. until 1943, and was then transferred to the Command and General Staff School at Forth Leavenworth, Kansas. After graduation I was assigned to the 95th Infantry Division at Fort Sam Houston, Texas. My next orders instructed me to report to Headquarters, Third

Army also at Fort Sam Houston. I was made Chief of

Test and Inspection Section. Our mission was to

visit units in eight southwestern states to determine

their training status. At Fort Clark, Texas, for

example, our team composed of infantry, artillery,

engineer and medical officers conducted a series of

basic tests. One of the tests given the 2nd Cavalry

Division was on physical fitness. We named it the

"Joe Louis Test." He was the heavyweight champion

of the world and it motivated the soldiers to do well.

On January 1, 1944, our Third Army

Headquarters was alerted to go overseas. We took

the train from San Antonio, Texas to Camp Shanks,

New York, ready to embark for a place and

commander unknown to us at the time. Shortly after

our arrival at Camp Shanks, however, a letter arrived at our postal unit from Mrs. Patton addressed to "Lieutenant General George S. Patton, Jr., Commanding General, Third United States Army." In a matter of minutes, all of us knew that our new boss was going to be "Old Blood and Guts."

Our trip across the Atlantic was on the *Isle de France*, a former French luxury liner. It had been converted into a troop transport ship. It was not an enjoyable experience, as we had to zigzag our way across the Atlantic to avoid a submarine attack. Quarters were cramped and the food left much to be desired.

We disembarked in Scotland on March 5, 1944 and a day later arrived in Knutsford, England. Field grade officers were billed with families in the

community.

GENERAL PATTON
ASSUMES COMMAND

We met General Patton (Figure 1-1) the following day at nearby Camp Peover (Figure 1-2). He greeted us with the words I quoted in my opening remarks: "Remember, I'm not here." We didn't know what those four words meant at that time, but later in his talk he emphasized, "You'll understand at a future date what I meant and why you cannot disclose why I am here and that I am your commander." Willie, his newly acquired bull terrier remained at his side during the entire talk. We all came to know his beloved dog quite well. Willie became the constant companion of Patton from March 1944 until Patton's death in December 1945 (Figure 1-3).

As a member of the Operations Division and former Chief of the Test and Inspection Section, I had an opportunity to observe Patton frequently. He would visit various units throughout England, Northern Ireland, and Scotland where the incoming Third Army troops were assembled and trained. He would inspire them with his motivational talks (Figure 1-4) that only my boss could do in his inimitable style. During the time we were in the Knutsford area, I became a briefing officer and would inform General Patton and the staff on plans for the invasion of Europe – the overall plan was called Overlord (Figure 1-5).

Figure 1-1 Favorite World War II photo
General Patton spent many years practicing what he called his "fighting face." He also dressed to portray the image of a rough, tough warrior.

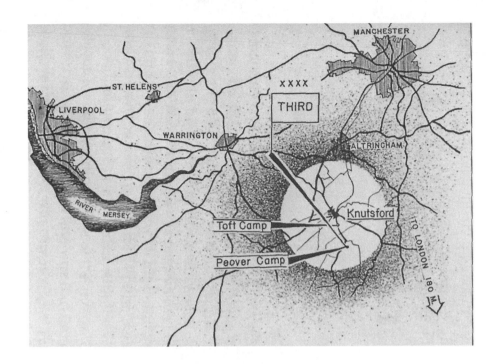

Figure 1-2 Camp Peover

Our first home with Patton was at Camp Peover, located outside Knutsford. Here he greeted us with, "Remember, I'm not here."

Figure 1-3 General Patton and Willie

General Patton and his beloved dog, Willie. He accompanied Patton everywhere from the time the General acquired him in March 1944 until his death in December 1945. This photo was taken in Nancy, France. Note that Patton and Willie share center stage, surrounded by senior Third Army officers.

Patton's Address to His Troops

NOW I WANT YOU TO REMEMBER THAT NO BASTARD EVER WON A WAR BY DYING FOR HIS COUNTRY. YOU WON IT BY MAKING THE OTHER DUMB BASTARD DIE FOR HIS COUNTRY. Men, all this stuff you've heard about America not wanting to fight, wanting to stay out of the war, is a lot of horse dung. Americans traditionally love to fight. All REAL Americans, love the sting of battle. When you were kids, you all admired the champion marble shooter, the fastest runner, the big league ball players, the toughest boxers . . . Americans love a winner and will not tolerate a loser. Americans play to win all the time. I wouldn't give a hoot in Hell for a man who lost and laughed. That's why Americans have never lost and will never lose a war. Because the very thought of losing is hateful to Americans. Now, an army is a team. It lives, eats, sleeps, fights as a team. This individuality stuff is a bunch of crap. The biggest bastards who wrote that stuff about individuality for the Saturday Evening Post, don't know anything more about real battle than they do about fornicating. Now we have the finest food and equipment, the best spirit, and the best men in the world. You know . . . my God, I actually pity those poor bastards we're going up against. My God, I do. We're not just going to shoot the bastards, we're going to cut out their living guts and use them to grease the treads of our tanks. We're going to murder those lousy Hun bastards by the bushel. Now some of you boys, I know, are wondering whether or not you'll chicken out under fire. Don't worry about it. I can assure you that you'll all do your duty. The Nazis are the enemy. Wade into them. Spill their blood, shoot them in the belly. When you put your hand into a bunch of goo, that a moment before was your best friend's face, you'll know what to do. Now there's another thing I want you to remember. I don't want to get any messages saying that we are holding our position. We're not holding anything, we'll let the Hun do that. We are advancing constantly, and we're not interested in holding onto anything except the enemy. We're going to hold onto him by the nose, and we're going to kick him in the ass. We're going to kick the hell out of him all the time, and we're going to go through him like crap through a goose. Now, there's one thing that you men will be able to say when you get back home, and you may thank God for it. Thirty years from now when you're sitting around your fireside with your grandson on your knee, and he asks you, "What did you do in the great World War Two?" You won't have to say, "Well, I shoveled shit in Louisiana." Alright now, you sons of bitches, you know how I feel. Oh! . . . I will be proud to lead you wonderful guys in battle anytime, anywhere. That's all.

— General George S. Patton, Jr.

Figure 1-4 Patton Talk to His Troops

Prior to combat, Patton would visit troops under his command and give motivational talks. He used no notes and no exact record was kept of them. He varied his speeches slightly and here is one of them. He was an outstanding speaker.

13

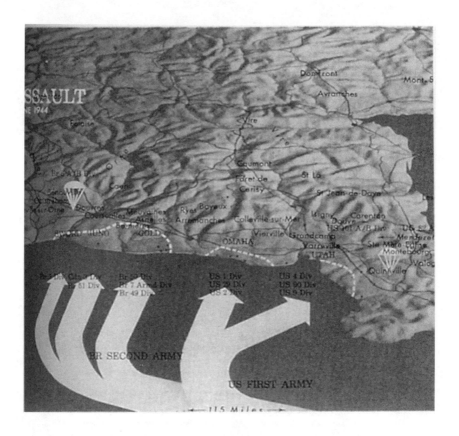

Figure 1-5 Assault Area

This map portrays the actual assault area that was code named Operation Overlord. The landings began June 6, 1944. Fortitude was a sub-plan within Overlord.

Source: Report by the Supreme Commander to the Combined Chiefs of Staff on the Operation in Europe of the Allied Expeditionary Force in Europe, 6 June 1944 - 8 May 1945, p. 20.

14

FORTITUDE

Within the total plan was a sub-plan called

"Fortitude." This deception concept had as its

purpose to lead the enemy forces to believe that

Patton was going to be the commander of an Army

Group that was going to invade France in the Pas de

Calais region. This fictitious Allied Force composed

of two Armies and their supporting units commanded

by General Patton was located in southeast England

(Figure 1-6). The Germans kept eighteen divisions in

the Pas de Calais region of France to guard against

Patton's invasion. And those troops included some

of their best armor divisions with ample numbers of

Panther and Tiger Tanks.

Why did the German High Command fear

Patton? Because he was highly respected for his

battlefield accomplishments in Sicily, as an Army

Commander, and in North Africa as the leader of the

Western Task Force. The Nazis also recognized that

Patton was the "fightingest" soldier in the United

States Army. They knew that Patton had fought

successfully in the Punitive Expedition in Mexico

(Figure 1-7) under General Pershing and

commanded a tank brigade in World War I

(Figure 1-8).

A visit to Patton's fictitious Army Group, in

southeast England, gave the impression that a

mighty combat force was being assembled to launch

an all-out attack. It included personnel, vehicles,

tanks, artillery, ships, planes and a communication

network. Upon closer examination it was apparent

that much of the equipment was fake. An officer on

General Bradley's staff involved in Operation Fortitude went back to the states and worked with tire and toy manufacturers to make rubber tanks, vehicles, and other equipment that could be inflated. The British produced similar fake items to include tanks (Figure 1-9) and vehicles (Figure 1-10). United Kingdom craftsmen also created what they called Rupert (Figure 1-11) - dropped from airplanes they appeared to be paratroopers.

The Germans, in their flyovers and by intercepted messages, thought they had uncovered the real McCoy. The Allies did sprinkle actual equipment in the area. Patton was sighted frequently in the Dover area. Fortitude proved to be a marvelous subterfuge. A National D-Day Museum plaque reads in part as follows:

17

The main objective of Allied deception strategy was to convince the Germans that an invasion would indeed take place - but not at Normandy.   The most obvious choice for an invasion site was Calais, located at the narrowest part of the English Channel, only 22 miles from Great Britain. Hitler was almost certain the Allies would attack here. The Allies encouraged Hitler's belief by employing an ingenious ruse. Throughout southeastern England they built phony armies, complete with dummy planes, ships, tanks and jeeps. With the help of British and American motion picture crews, they created entire Army bases that would look authentic to German reconnaissance aircraft. These "bases" gave the impression of a massive Allied buildup in preparation for an invasion of France at Calais.

When the Allies did invade Normandy, June 6, 1944, Hitler held his divisions in the Pas de Calais region, fearing Patton would launch the major attack from the Dover area. Hitler did not release the armor units until it was too late to repel the Allied forces at Normandy. If General Rommel, commander of the enemy troops at Normandy, had been granted permission to use the Panzer divisions, Eisenhower's troops might have been pushed back into the sea. But Hitler feared Patton and his Phantom Army Group so no reinforcements were made available until it was too late.

Patton's Third Army became operational August 1, 1944. Shortly thereafter, the Third Army was advancing rapidly on four fronts - toward Brest, Paris, the Loire River, and Falaise (Figure 1-12).

Figure 1-6 Fortitude Location

This map includes Southeast England and the Pas de Calais region of France. This is the area in Europe where General Patton's fictitious First U.S. Army Group (FUSAG) was located, as well as the region in France where the Allies planned to attack. Note the short distance from Dover and Margate to the Pas de Calais versus Southampton to the Normandy beaches.

Figure 1-7   Punitive Expedition, Mexico (1916-1917)
Patton received his first national publicity for his combat
exploits in killing several of the enemy.

Figure 1-8 Patton and Tank, World War I

Patton set a fine soldierly example for his troops. At the time
he was a Lt. Colonel posing with a tank of World War I
vintage. A few months later he was promoted to Colonel -
age 32.

Figure 1-9 Rubber Tank
British soldiers lift an inflated dummy tank. The Allies built
fake vehicles and army bases to deceive the Germans about
the true invasion location.
Source: Photo and inscription, The National D-Day Museum

Figure 1-10 British Army Vehicle

A British soldier stands beside one of the many fake vehicles that were deployed in southeast England as part General Patton's fictitious Army Group.

Source: Photo and inscription, The National D-Day Museum

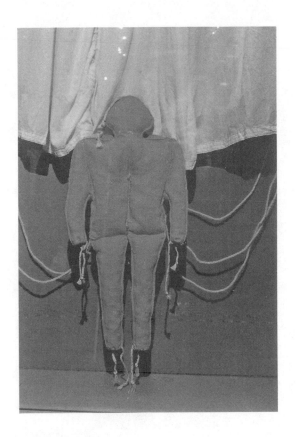

Figure 1-11 Rupert

One of the most unusual deceptions for D-Day involved
hundreds of these dummy paratroopers, known as "Ruperts."
Early on D-Day morning they were dropped with several real
paratroopers east of the invasion zone, in Normandy and the
Pas de Calais. The dummies were dressed in paratrooper
uniforms, complete with boots and helmets. To create the
illusion of a large airborne drop, the dummies were equipped
with recordings of gunfire and exploding mortar rounds. The
real troops would supply additional special effects, including
flares, chemicals to simulate the smell of exploded shells, and
amplified battle sounds. This operation, codenamed "Titanic"
was designed to distract and confuse German forces while the
main airborne forces landed farther to the west.
Source: Photo and inscription, The National D-Day Museum

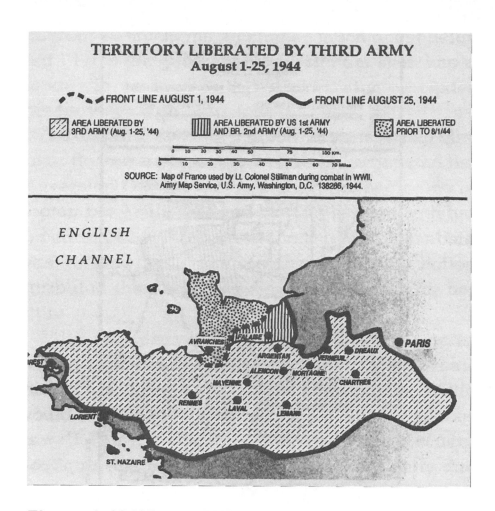

Figure 1-12 What a Difference 25 Days Made!

Copyright © 2004 Richard J. Stillman. All Rights Reserved
Note the territory taken by Third Army in its explosive
breakout after becoming operational on August 1, 1944.
Willie frequently accompanied Patton as the General visited
combat units and the Fortitude area.

ULTRA

I indicated earlier that Fortitude was part of Overlord, the overall plan for the total defeat of enemy forces in Europe. There was another aspect of Allied ingenuity that proved invaluable. Churchill referred to it as, "My most secret source." This intelligence information was code-named "Ultra." The Germans named their code machine "Enigma" (Figure 1-13). It was so complex that Hitler and the German High Command thought that it was invincible. But thanks to a brilliant team of primarily British mathematicians and cryptographers the code was broken. This was accomplished just prior to World War II. British intelligence was able to intercept and decode top-secret radio messages from Hitler and his senior commanders. This form of

intelligence was obtained throughout World War II.

Figure 1-13 Enigma
How *did* Enigma Work?

Despite the complex system of wires, plugs, and ciphering wheels, the Enigma machine was fairly simple to use. The operator just typed the letters of a message – the machine's internal mechanisms did the rest. Pressing a key (1) sent an electrical current through the plug board wiring (2) and activated the wheels (3). The wheels rotated to produced an encrypted letter, which lit up above the keyboard. The code changed according to the wheel and plug position. Each configuration produced a different scrambled letter. To read or write a coded message, the operator wrote down all of the letters as they lit up. Operators were given monthly charts to indicate the daily settings, because a message enciphered by an Enigma machine could be deciphered only by another Enigma machine with the same setting.

Source: Photo and inscription, the National D-Day Museum. (The machine is located in the Deception Area.)

Patton received his first Ultra briefing as commander of the Western Task Force in North Africa. It made him a believer in this form of intelligence. He recognized that Ultra was a remarkable tool. It gave him, he said, "prompt information of the enemies' intentions," based on intercepting the messages that were sent by Hitler and his generals. But along with the Ultra information, Patton knew that he also needed to have other intelligence sources such as agents working behind enemy lines, good intelligence analysis, and visits to the front lines by himself and members of his staff. Patton pointed out that, "Only with this total intelligence overview can I make sound combat decisions."

In summary, Fortitude and Ultra played significant roles in achieving Allied victories in World War II. But it was leaders like my old boss General George S. Patton, Jr. and the soldiers, sailors, airmen and their commanders who won the war.

OTHER DECEPTION PLANS

There were other deception plans but none had the success of Fortitude. A map listing the plans along with comments appears in a Museum display (Figure 1-14). Those of us at Patton's Headquarters knew about the other deceptions but were concentrating our efforts on planning for the Third Army's combat role in Normandy (code named Overlord).

FRENCH CONTRIBUTION

The French resistance forces also played a helpful role prior to the invasion. An example of the resistance work appears in Figure 1-15. Equipment used to maintain contact included tiny radios (Figure 1-16). The French forces under General Charles

DeGaulle grew in size as the Allies became stronger and were winning victories on the battlefield.

DeGaulle was a thorn in the side of the Allied High Command to include Prime Minister Churchill and President Roosevelt. He expected his initially small French forces to be treated equal to the U.S.S.R., U.S.A., and U.K. In fact, however, he only had a minority of French who supported him. The rest were loyal to Petain and his Vichy Regime that worked with the Nazis and sent volunteer troops to fight on the German eastern front. When General DeGaulle came to visit our Third Army Headquarters at Knutsford, England, Patton commented after he left, *"DeGaulle departed leaving many a dry eye behind."* (Source: Stillman's *General Patton's Timeless Leadership Principles,* p.10)

Figure 1-14. False Landing Sites

For Overlord to succeed, the Allies had to keep German forces dispersed throughout Europe so that no additional troops could be dispatched to Normandy. To do this, they provided misinformation to double agents and arranged intelligence "leaks" to suggest preparations for invasions at various sites. Phony radio traffic and fake tanks, aircraft, and military installations created illusionary invasion armies. The deception scheme was code-named "Fortitude." The main element was Operation Quicksilver, which effectively held down German divisions in the Pas de Calais. But German intelligence also learned of possible invasions planned for Norway (Operation Skye), southern France (Operation Vendetta), Western France (Operation Ironside), and Greece (Operation Turpitude). These other schemes weren't very effective. Only Operation Skye worried Hitler, who kept Norway heavily defended.

Source: The National D-Day Museum (Deception Plans Exhibit Area)

34

Figure 1-15 Sabotage by Resistance Forces
One of the useful missions the French provided after the Allies landed in Normandy was to destroy railroad tracks as indicated in this photograph.
Source: The National D-Day Museum (Deception Plans Exhibit Area)

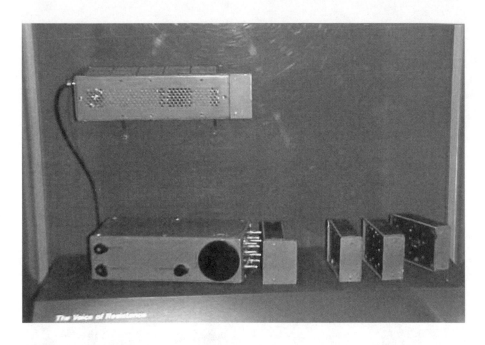

Figure 1-16 Radios used by Resistance Groups

Resistance groups throughout German-occupied Europe relied on small radios like this one to receive coded messages from the Allies. Because possession of a radio or receiver was grounds for imprisonment, resistance agents needed radios that could easily be concealed. Receivers were hidden in all sorts of innocent-looking items, including books and food containers. This MCR-1 (Miniature Communications Receiver Km 1) "biscuit tin" radio fit into a small cookie box. The British SOE (Special Operations executive) issued many of these portable radio sets to their agents and French resistance groups.

Source: Photo and inscription, The National D-Day Museum (Deception Plans Exhibit Area), Gift of Kenneth W. Rendell.

FOOTNOTE TO HISTORY

I was a member of the faculty at the NATO Defense College in Paris from 1960 to 1963. I came to admire DeGaulle for his vision in recognizing that the French colonies in North Africa should have their independence. It was a time of turmoil in France with DeGaulle supporters on one side and the old Vichy supporters on the other. There were a number of attempts to assassinate him. One was on his visit to the Ecole Militare, where the NATO Defense College was located.

On Friday morning February 15th, I arrived at the NATO Defense College and noted substantial extra security around the entire Ecole Militare. The building housed not only the NATO Defense College, which occupied one wing, but also the entire French senior military school system. I inquired from a French military guard who protected our College, as to what was happening.

He told me that General DeGaulle would be speaking to the graduating class and presenting diplomas to them. When I was informed that DeGaulle would arrive shortly, I decided to observe his arrival and possibly shake his hand. As I walked through the interior courtyard, I had an eerie feeling that something was wrong. Little did I realize that French armed guards with telescopic-sight rifles were located on the rooftop of the building. I realized later that being in civilian clothes I could have been easily shot as a person plotting to kill the President of France. However, I made it to the arrival site and observed a large gathering of French military. As

DeGaulle stepped from his car, I attempted to shake his hand, but was interceded by a French officer. He inquired, "What are you doing here?" I explained my diplomatic status and said I would like to shake the General's hand. The officer informed me that it would not be possible and to return immediately to the NATO Defense College.

I learned that evening about the plot to kill DeGaulle and read all about it in the paper later. I also found out that the security in the area was so tight because a French lady on our NATO staff was reportedly involved in the plot.[1]

---

[1] I related this attempt to kill DeGaulle in my scrap book (My tour in Europe). It included a copy of the New York Herald Tribune (European Edition dated Sat-Sun February 16-17, 1963). The front page of the Tribune headlined: "Plot to kill DeGaulle smashed; 3 officers and woman arrested." The subtitled stated, "Attack set at military school with a telescopic sight rifle." The article said that a plot by French Army officers to assassinate President Charles DeGaulle this morning in the courtyard of the Ecole Militare was smashed in a series of overnight arrests by French security police.

One final thought. On March 6, 1963 General DeGaulle's son Philipe DeGaulle visited our NATO Defense College to hear a lecture by the French General d'Armee F. R. Beaufry. His topic was Modern Weapons and Strategy. Philipe sat next to me and we had a nice chat. At the time he was a French Naval Captain assigned to the NATO desk in the French Ministry.

WHERE WAS GENERAL PATTON?

The National D-Day Museum (New Orleans, LA) was opened with great fanfare on June 6, 2000. The date itself was significant as 46 years earlier the Allies initially landed in Normandy, France. The Museum held a five-day celebration (June 3-7, 2000) that included a major parade, dinner, dance and speeches by dignitaries, such as Secretary of Defense William Cohen, Tom Hanks, Tom Brokaw, Major General Livingston (local Marine Corps Medal of Honor recipient) and Steven Spielberg.

It was my good fortune to attend all the festivities and talk with Tom Hanks, Tom Brokaw and fellow veterans. To assure my having a ringside view of all activities, I provided funds for an exhibit in one section of the Museum that displays deception plans of the Allies as well as equipment. To my dismay, however, there were no photos or mention of my old boss, General Patton. Fortunately, I was able to contact Dr. Stephen E. Ambrose, my longtime colleague at the University of New Orleans and the driving force behind the Museum's establishment. I suggested to Steve, and his best friend, Dr. Gordon H. "Nick" Mueller, that General Patton be recognized for his significant role in the success of the Fortitude deception plan.

Both agreed that Figures 1-17 and 17a present the deception entrance and the Patton display. I also received a kind letter from Dr. Ambrose (Figure 1-18) as well as a letter from Dr. Mueller to Tom Brokaw in regard to my book on Patton's leadership principles that was sent to him after his visit to New Orleans (Figure 1-19).

One of the activities held at the Museum's opening was a seminar in regard to D-Day by veterans who participated. I spoke to the audience about General Patton's contributions. Other dignitaries on the state were General Andrew Goodpaster (Former NATO Commander), Senator George McGovern and several military veterans who landed in Normandy on D-Day (Figure 1-20).

A font page story in the June 6, 2000 edition of the Times-Picayune read in part "the glittering new National D-Day Museum pays tribute to young Americans who turned the tide of World War II, but on Monday, it was aging hero's who took center stage and quietly and compelling and told their stories."

It has made me happy to see the enthusiastic response to our National D-Day Museum. A million people have visited the Museum in its first three years of existence. I am particularly pleased to see the great interest in the exhibit of my old boss General Patton.

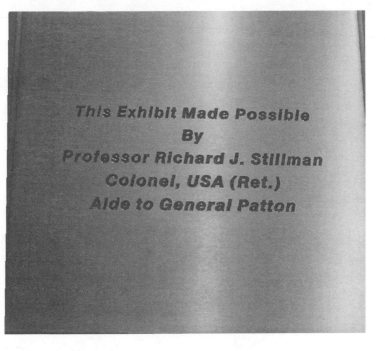

Figure 1-17 Deception Area Entrance

The inscription and photo shown here appear at the entrance
to the deception exhibits.
Source: The National D-Day Museum

Figure 1-17a General Patton and Lieutenant Colonel Stillman

The inscription and photo shown here appear at the entrance to the deception exhibits.

Source: The National D-Day Museum

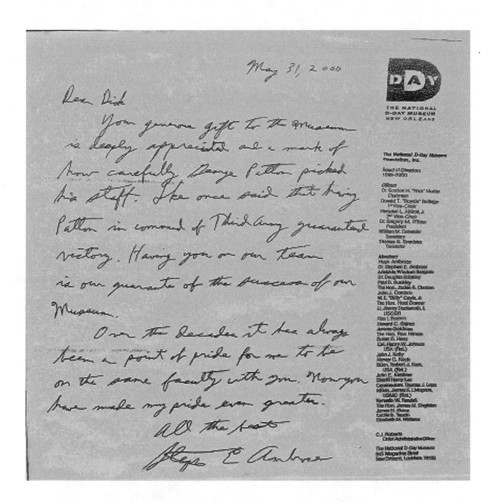

Figure 1-18 Ambrose Thank You Letter

This letter from Dr. Ambrose, my colleague at the University of New Orleans, is a treasured memento. He had invited me to speak at the Eisenhower Center on a number of occasions. At the end of my talks on Patton, I emphasized that my old boss would go down in history as "the greatest combat commander America has ever produced." Steve's comments would be: "Well at least Richard Stillman thinks so." We must remember that Ambrose was Eisenhower's biographer. In my view, there is a tendency of historians who know their subjects well to become supporters and admirers.

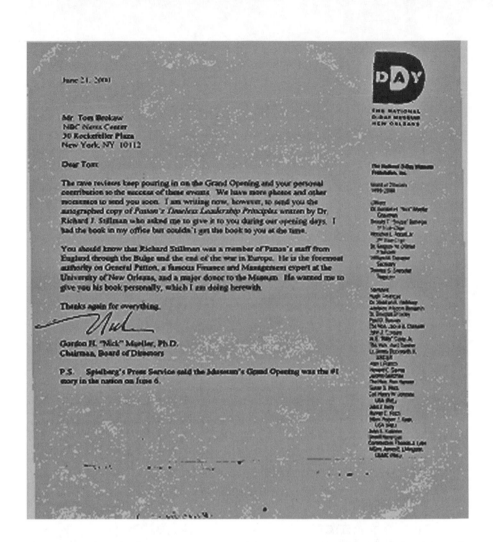

Figure 1-19 Autographed Patton Leadership Book

I had hoped to give my Patton Leadership Book personally to
Tom Brokaw. Unfortunately, this did not happen. I spoke with
Brokaw on the elevator at the hotel and during the cocktail
hour. He commented, "General Patton is my hero."

CONVERSATIONS WITH VETERANS

THE SOLDIERS OF THE SECOND WORLD WAR

Riverside Hilton New Orleans, Ballrooms A, B, and C

9:30 a.m. – 5:30 p.m.
Monday, June 6, 2000

Presented by The Eisenhower Center for American *Studies, University of New Orleans*

Music by the 156th U.S. Army National Guard Band
Presentation of flags by the Joint Service Color Guard

Panelists:

- **Ambassador George McGovern**
  15th Air Force, B-24 Pilot
- General Andrew Goodpaster
  Former NATO Commander
- **Dr. Richard J. Stillman**
  Member of GEN George S Patton, Jr.'s Staff, "Operation Fortitude"
- **J. Robert "Bob" Slaughter**
  29th Infantry Division, 116th Infantry Regiment
- **Leonard "Len" Lomell**
  2nd Ranger Battalion, Company D
- **Senator John Willie "Bulldog" Drummond**
  USAAF P-47 Pilot, POW taken near St Lo
- **Alan Reeves**
  National Commander SIIAEF
- **Marguerite Guthrie Boyd**
  U.S. Army Nurse Corps
- **Ralph Gorenson**
  29th Infantry Division, 116th Infantry Regiment

Figure 1-20 Presentations by World War II Veterans

Panelists who gave presentations at the Hilton Hotel in New Orleans on June 6, 2000. Dr Stephen E. Ambrose was the moderator. The entire presentation was aired on C-SPAN on July 7, 2000.

VICTORY BALL

I was delighted to attend the Third Annual Victory Ball, June 6, 2003, at the invitation of my friend, Ambassador Lindy Boggs, who is a member of the Museum Board of Trustees. The highlight of the evening was the presentation, by General H. Norman Schwartzkof (Figure 1-21) of the first "American Spirit Award" to Dr. Ambrose. The objective of the award is as follows:

The American Spirit Award recognizes that individual who best exemplifies the outstanding qualities of the American Spirit, including teamwork, optimism, courage, and sacrifice, and expression of these values through their own life and actions. The First American Spirit Award recipient is Dr. Stephen E. Ambrose, whose life and works were dedicated to the values exemplified by the heroes of American History who he loved and wrote about. Dr. Ambrose's work reflects what it means to be an American. Through his vision and commitment, Dr. Ambrose led a group of friends and colleagues to found the country's premier museum of World War II, The National D-Day Museum, which opened its doors three years ago in New Orleans. This outstanding facility, which is dedicated to the mission of celebrating the American Spirit, stands as a testament to the leadership and optimisms of Dr. Ambrose and to his ability to provide vision for others through his life and actions. His family, his stories and the Museum are part of his incredible legacy.

Figure 1-21 General H. Norman Schwartzkof
Photo of General H. Norman Schwartzkof, Dr. Richard J.
Stillman and Ambassador Lindy Boggs taken at the Victory
Ball, June 6, 2003.

PART TWO

HOW THE HUNTINGTON LIBRARY OBTAINED THE NUREMBERG LAWS AND *MEIN KAMPF* FROM PATTON

The mystery of what happened to a rare edition of Hitler's book *Mein Kampf* and the Nuremberg Laws was revealed in the media over a half century after General Patton's death.

This section points out why the material Patton presented to the Huntington Library was kept secret.

BACKGROUND

"Library has Hitler-signed blue print of Holocaust." Front-page stories in many newspapers revealed information similar to what appeared in the *Times Picayune* (New Orleans), on June 26, 1999. The *Picayune* quoted Sharon Waxman (*Washington Post*) as follows: "For 54 years a document of immense historical moment was buried unknown and unseen in the inner vault of a small American museum." The article went on to point out that "not even Holocaust scholars knew that the Nuremberg Laws - the original M221 Code of racial discrimination - was hidden in the Huntington Library in Pasadena, California since 1945, a gift from General Patton to a friend and neighbor."

The primary reason that Patton selected the

Huntington Library was the long time relationship that the Patton's had with the Huntington's. They lived close to each other in the affluent section of Pasadena, California. At one time Patton's father managed the Huntington Property. The photograph (Figure 2-1) shows the Patton's and Mr. Huntington together in 1904. Young George Patton was a cadet at the Virginia Military Institute and had returned home to take a test given by his Senator for admission to the United States Military Academy (West Point, NY).

A visit by the author to the grounds and library, in 1948, was a delightful experience. It is beautifully maintained and Patton made a wise decision in selecting Huntington for his documents.

Newspaper headlines, in June 1999, revealed

the fact that General Patton had given the Huntington

Library, in Pasadena, California two significant

documents. Patton, in June 1945, had presented the

Director of Huntington both a rare copy of *Mein*

Kampf and the original copy of the Nuremberg Laws

(Figure 2-2).

Figure 2-1 Patton Family
This photo was taken at the Patton Family home in Pasadena, California (Feb. 1904). Left to right: Sister Nita, GSP, Jr., (in Virginia Military Institute Uniform), Patton's mother, and Patton's father and Mr. Henry E. Huntington.

Figure 2-2 Patton at the Henry E. Huntington Library and Art Gallery

This photo shows General Patton presenting the copy of *Mein Kampf* to Robert Millikan, Chairman of the Library. It was done during Patton's visit to the United States in June 1945. Note the pose under the painting of General George Washington, the Father of our Country. Patton was a master at maximizing public opportunities on every occasion. I am sure, however, he didn't realize the type of reaction it would receive 54 years after the photo was taken.

Why did the "discovery" of these two documents, 54 years after the Patton death, cause such a furor?

I have spent considerable time, study and research, since 1997, to find answers to that question. The project could not have been completed without the fine assistance from four sources:

- **Martin E. Dannenberg**: He was the Special Agent in Charge of the 203rd Counter Intelligence Corps (CIC) that was assigned to III Corps (part of Third Army). It was Dannenberg who traced down the original copy of the Laws. After World War II he returned to the Sunlife Insurance Companies and later became President and Chief Executive Officer.

- **Roger E. Lawless**: A comrade in arms since our days at the NATO Defense College (Paris, France) in 1960. After a career in the military, Colonel Lawless had a successful law practice in Los Angeles, California. As a local Patton admirer he has kept me posted on events regarding my old boss appearing in various publications.

- **Michael G. Gretchen**: Longtime Executive Vice President, Hibernia National Bank, invites me to speak on my favorite subject and sends me valuable Patton information.

- **Huntington Library**: The staff has been an important source in regard to its knowledge of the *Mein Kampf* copy and Nuremberg Laws.

The story about the Patton gifts came to light as the result of a friendship that developed between Robert Skotheim, President of the Huntington Library and Uri Herscher, President of the Skirball Cultural Center. The *Times Picayune*, New Orleans, a major daily newspaper had a front page headline (June 26, 1999) announcing that, "Library has Hitler signed blueprint of Holocaust." The article reads, in part, as follows:

> "**LOS ANGELES** – For 54 years, a document of immense historical moment was buried, unknown and unseen, in the inner vault of a small American museum.
> Not even Holocaust scholars knew that the Nuremberg Laws – the original Nazi code of racial discrimination against Jews that was drafted over a weekend in 1935, signed by Adolf Hitler and

sealed with bright red swastikas – were hidden at the Huntington Library in Pasadena, California since 1945, a gift from General George Patton to a friend and neighbor.

Now a friendship between two scholars from two different worlds will result in the document's public display. Starting next week, the laws that helped set the Holocaust in motion will go on view at a Jewish Cultural Center in Los Angeles, along with a lavish edition of Hitler's political treatise "*Mein Kampf*" that also belonged to Patton." (Article by Sharon Waxman –The *Washington Post*)

NUREMBERG LAWS AND DANNENBERG'S ROLE

As the media highlighted, in 1999, there were two gifts that Patton gave to Huntington – *Mein Kampf* book and the Nuremberg Laws. In regard to the book, some of us on Patton's staff had heard rumors about *Mein Kampf* being in Patton's possession, but our concerns were about winning the war and going home to our families. Let us first look at details on how the Nuremberg Laws were discovered.

❖ What role did Martin E. Dannenberg play in regard to the Laws?

I first contacted Mr. Dannenberg after reading the article that appeared in the *Times Picayune* by Sharon Waxman. After our conversation, the following appeared in the *Baltimore Sun*. It explains Dannenberg's significant role, in the discovery of the "Laws".

"Sharon Waxman's front-page story concerning the discovery of the infamous "Nuremberg Laws" in the Huntington Library in Pasadena Calif. needs some revision. I was the special agent in charge of the 203rd Counter-Intelligence Corps (CIC) detachment, assigned to the III Corps, a part of Gen. Patton's Third Army. While working on an assignment in Regensburg, we apprehended a mid-level Nazi official who informed us of the location of an important document, known as the "Nuremberg Degrees" stored in the vault of a bank in the town of Eischstatt.

The document had been given to the mayor of Nuremberg for safekeeping. He passed it on to the security chief of the Waffen SS, who was instructed to deliver it to Hans Ruch, an official of the France Ministry, who selected the Eischstatt bank vault. I asked my prisoner how he knew all of this. Dr. Ruch, he said, was his uncle who lived on a farm near Eischstatt.

With Dr. Ruch's help, CIC agents J. Maxwell Pickens of Bessemer, Ala., and Military Intelligence interpreter Frank J. Perls of Los Angeles and I located two bank officials who could open the vault. In a box we found an envelope sealed with red swastika embossments. I extracted the documents slowly, and there was Adolf Hitler's and three other signatures, dooming Jews to the nightmare of the Holocaust. To document the event, I took photos with my Minox spy camera, and I have a shot of Frank Perls and me holding the documents, taken in the vault.

I reported our find to the III Corps intelligence chief, Col. B. I. Homer, who didn't seem to attach much importance to the find but nevertheless instructed me to report it to the SHAEF (Supreme Headquarters, Allied Expeditionary Force) document people, who were collecting evidence for the expected trial of war criminals. I was told to turn over the documents to Gen. Patton's intelligence chief for delivery to SHAEF. It is evident that Gen. Patton never sent them on to Paris but retained them as a personal souvenir that made its way into the Huntington Library, as The Post reported. (Martin Dannenberg – *Baltimore*)"

Photos of Martin E. Dannenberg and the Laws were mailed to me (Figure 2-3). In his letter, Dannenberg said: "I am enclosing several photos. Unfortunately we had no lights other than poor lighting in the bank. I used a Minox camera. Small flash equipment had not yet been invented. One of the photos is Perls, the interpreter assigned to me by

III Corps' MII Team, (he's the one on the right) and

me (on the left holding the document). It was taken

in the bank by Art Pickens. I had just slit open the

envelope and extracted the papers. I then placed the

documents on the table and photographed the two

pages."

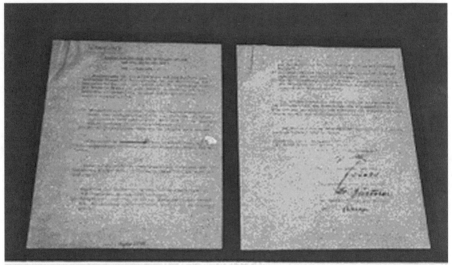

Figure 2-3 Martin E Dannenberg and the "Laws"

These photos were taken the day Dannenberg discovered the original copy of the Nuremberg Laws

General Patton's account of how he acquired the Nuremberg Laws differs from Dannenberg's. Here is what the General dictated at the Huntington Library in June 1945. Also note his comment on the *Mein Kampf* copy.

"When the Third Army entered the city of Nuremberg there was quite a fight going on, the city was burning. Some troops of the 90th Infantry Division fighting through the town came to a stairway, which they went down with grenades, in case there were any Germans. There were no Germans. They found a vault, not open, and persuaded a German to open it for them. In it they found this thing. That was <u>all</u> that was in the vault.

These soldiers of the 90th Division were very fond of me and I was very fond of them. They thought they would like to do something for me, so they sent for me, and we had a great public presentation. The former commanding general of the 90th Division, now commander of the Third Corps, General Van Fleet, - he actually made the presentation to me. So it is my property. They have given me a lot of other things but this is the important one. This [document] was taken the day we captured Nuremberg, about the 14th of March. We captured so many towns I have forgotten just which day. The presentation must have been about the 27th of May."

Regarding *Mein Kampf*

"That book was alleged by a talkative German to be one of a limited edition of the unexpurgated text. There were alleged to have been one hundred copies. It was published by a man named Amman. He is the No. 3 bad man in Germany. I have him in jail now. We'll stretch him pretty quick." (Huntington Library. San Marino, Calif., June 11, 1945)

Patton mentioned Max Amman as the publisher of *Mein Kampf* and No. 3 in Hitler's hierarchy. Actually Amman was the publisher of Hitler's propaganda material. While our Third Army Headquarters was in Bad Tolz, I was invited to General Patton's residence located at Tegernsee. It had been the home of Max Amman and truly a luxurious estate.

❖ How did the Nuremberg Laws and *Mein Kampf* move from the Huntington to Skirball?

On June 28, 1999 the Huntington Library and the Skirball Cultural Center made a joint press release. This release was quoted in major newspapers and other media. I have included the release in its entirely because of the historical significance.

"HUNTINGTON LIBRARY TO LOAN ORIGINAL NUREMBERG LAWS SIGNED BY HITLER TO THE SKIRBALL CULTURAL CENTER

Los Angles – The original text of the Nuremberg laws bearing Hitler's signature will be loaned by the Huntington Library to the Skirball Cultural Center for an indefinite period, Huntington President Robert A. Skotheim announced. The Huntington will also place on loan a deluxe edition of Hitler's *Mein Kampf* whose nightmarish vision was realized in the Nuremberg decrees. The laws and the book were both presented to General George S. Patton Jr. by his troops in 1945, and were later given to The Huntington by the General, along with correspondence from the General to the Huntington concerning all of these materials. When President Skotheim visited the Skirball several months ago with Skirball President Uri D. Herscher, Skotheim was particularly struck by the story told there. *This*, Skotheim said, would be the appropriate venue in which to exhibit the Hitler related materials given to the Huntington by General Patton.

The Nuremberg Laws

The Nuremberg laws were a critical step initiating the Nazi Holocaust. The three typewritten documents that are being loaned are each signed by Hitler and dated September 15, 1935. Major General

73

J. A. Van Fleet in his letter to Patton transmitting the documents states that they are the original Nuremberg Laws. The decrees include: "Law for the Safeguard of German Blood of German Honor" prohibiting marriage, cohabitation, and relations between "Aryans" and Jews; "The Reich Citizen Law" defining a citizen of the German Reich as "of German … blood"; and "The Reich Flag Law" defining the flag of the Nazi state. According to Professor Peter Loewenberg of UCLA's Department of History and Program in Political Psychology, "The Nuremberg Laws represent a major step in the increasing marginalization of Jews from German life. In order to carry out the program of The Final Solution, the target group first has to be marginalized, dehumanized, and removed from the code of citizenship. This is a critical moment. This legally excludes them. The next step is humiliation – Kristallnacht, 1938 – then the wearing of yellow stars, then deportation, and finally the death camps."

Mein Kampf

In a letter dated April 15, 1945 Patton wrote to the Chairman of The Huntington Board of Trustees saying, "I am sending under separate cover a de luxe edition of *Mein Kampf* which was captured by the XX Corps of the Third Army in the vicinity of Weimar. This book may have historical value, and it is with this idea that I am sending it to the Library as a slight tribute to the memory of my father." On June 7, 945 Huntington Board Chairman Robert A. Millikan wrote expressing the great appreciation of the Trustees for the edition of *Mein Kampf*.

Documents to be on view in Skirball's Renovated Permanent Exhibition
Visions and Values: Jewish Life from Antiquity to America

"The Huntington is a cultural research center with a manuscript, rare book, and art collections devoted to the history of Anglo-American," said Skotheim. The close family friendship of the Huntington's and the Patton's explains why General Patton gave these captured Nazi items to the Library in 1945, but they do not fall within the subject areas of scholarly research or public display of our institution." Skotheim continued, "It is therefore appropriate that they be exhibited at the Skirball Cultural Center, where they can be viewed in context."

The Skirball Cultural Center interprets the American Jewish experience by exploring intersections between American democratic values and the Jewish heritage through museum exhibitions and public programs. An emphasis is placed on the importance of the memory in both Jewish culture and American society. According to President Herscher, "No memory rooted in the twentieth century is more potent than the Nazi Holocaust. The Skirball is not alone in recognizing that the memory of the Holocaust imposes a moral obligation to caution us against the possibility of genocide, to be grateful for the answer democracy enables us to give genocide – and to preserve the record. General Patton no doubt had something of the sort in mind when he accepted some basic Nazi documents removed from Germany by U.S. soldiers and deposited them at The Huntington Library. Given the state of our world as this century nears its end, the General might well have agreed that the time has come to bring these materials to public attention, in the hope of attaching ourselves evermore firmly to our democratic promise.

"The Huntington Library has held the documents since Patton presented hem to Millikan," said Skotheim. "We are glad The Huntington has been able to preserve them until they could be exhibited in an appropriate venue," he continued. The documents will be on display to the public in the Skirball Cultural Center's permanent exhibition, *Visions and Values: Jewish Life from Antiquity to America* from June29 through September 5, 1999. Following the renovation and expansion of the *Visions and Values* galleries, they will be on permanent exhibition beginning December 1999.

"It is with thanks to The Huntington that these documents will go on view at the Skirball, giving us the opportunity at an American Jewish institution to refresh our memory of a cruel time and to seek insight into the human meaning of the Nazi catastrophe," said Herscher. "We'll also be commemorating one of America's finest achievements, the liberation of Europe from Hitler's genocidal grip. The documents meant to destroy the Jewish people and all hope of democracy, will be displayed at the Skirball to encourage visitors to remember that Hitler did not have the last word. The democratic faith has the last word."

Mr. Dannenberg was invited to be the keynote speaker at the Skirball Cultural Center (December

1999) at the initial display of the Patton gifts. On that occasion, he shared his story, of how he secured *The Laws*, with an audience of 500.

On February 26, 2000 he wrote me, that: "The Patton gifts to Huntington have been loaned permanently to the Skirball Cultural Center. Figure 2-4 presents the Nuremberg Laws exhibit. In the lower left corner of the exhibit, is the ceremonial edition of *Mein Kampf*. Inscribed on its cover is the statement: "Presented to the Huntington by George S. Patton, Jr." Mr. Dannenberg said: "As you know, the Laws were never actually presented to the Huntington, but stored in their vault for the General. He considered the document his personal property."

Figure 2-4 Patton's gifts to Huntington
Presently on display at the Skirball Cultural Center (Los Angeles, CA)

In further correspondence (Figure 2-5) with Mr.

Dannenberg he informed me of the handling of the

two presents to Huntington by General Patton. The

facts, as well as Dannenberg's conclusion, will never

be known, as the principals involved are no longer

alive.

In summary, this section on Patton's gifts to the

Huntington Library reflect his flair for intrigue, as well

as his appreciation of history, and his desire to be a

central figure in the happenings of the twentieth

century.

ROM : MARTIN E DANNENBERG PHONE NO. : 410 889 0234 Mar. 06 2000 05:13PM P1

FAX to- Col. Richard Stillman FAX #504-286-7630 3/6/00

Dear Richard- Just want to let you know your one page transmission came through sharp and clear. Thanks

Just to clear the record, when GSP "gave" the documents to Huntington, according to Bob Skotheim, the current director, they were being held in their vault for the return of GSP. He did not want them exhibited at the Huntington and the library Board followed his request. In fact, as Skotheim told me in December, they were never accessioned by the library until just this past year (1999) when all the media and other attention brought them to light.

By this action it seems to me Huntington did not want to be the owner of the papers but indicates they felt they were Patton's possession they were simply holding for him (his heirs). This is contrary to the handling of the ceremonial copy of "Mein Kampf" which was given to Huntington about the same time and was promptly accessioned in their records. It is my feeling that the sentiment of the times played a role in the simple storage aspect of this document as opposed to other nazi trophies he shipped home. Of course we will never really know.

Best regards,

Figure 2-5 Fax from Dannenberg to Dr. Stillman

PART THREE
WHERE (AND WHY) PATTON IS BURIED IN LUXEMBOURG CEMETERY?

The American Military Cemetery in Luxembourg is one of the most popular tourist sites in Europe. The fact that General Patton is buried there has added greatly to its luster. Few people, however, are familiar with the true history of this cemetery. This section provides the details and is based on my friendship with the first superintendent.

Personal Visits

I have made several visits to the American Military Cemetery located on the outskirts of Luxembourg City. Since serving with General Patton, 1944-45, I have given many talks on my old boss. Here is one of the most frequently asked question and my response[2]:

Is Patton buried in Arlington National Cemetery in Arlington, Virginia?

No. General Patton rests in the American Military Cemetery on the outskirts of Luxembourg City, Luxembourg. His family believed that he wished to be buried with those who fought with him in Europe. Burial was on December 24, 1945. His gravesite was

---

[2] Source: From my book titles *General Patton's Timeless Leadership Principals*, Pgs 189-192. Hard Cover, 2002

originally among the other 5,075 graves but was moved to its present location between two flagpoles at the head of the grave plots on March 19, 1947.

The cemetery, located on over 50 acres, is situated in a beautiful wooded area. A nondenominational white stone chapel is located near the entrance. Visitors numbering 250,000 annually come to this Cemetery.

Figure 3-1 Patton Burial Site
American Military Cemetery on the outskirts of Luxembourg City

SELECTION OF THE FIRST SUPERINTENDENT

What made Colonel Davis so well suited to be appointed the first superintendent of the American Military Cemetery in Luxembourg City? It is helpful to look at his background leading up to this appointment[3].

Robert Warren Davis was born April 23, 1913 in California. He was a cadet at the United States Military Academy from July 1, 1932 to June 12, 1936. Upon graduation he was commissioned a Second Lieutenant in the Signal Corps. Three years after graduation he attended the Signal Corps School and in 1942 was appointed to the General Staff Corps. Davis was promoted to First Lieutenant on June 12, 1939 and received a temporary promotion to Captain

---

[3] Source: Official Army Register July 1, 1943

effective February 1, 1942. Subsequent temporary promotions resulted in his being a full Colonel prior to the end of World War II.

As a highly respected senior officer, who was thoroughly familiar with the Cemetery grounds; the City of Luxembourg; various local officials; knowledge of the language and customs; and his leadership abilities made Colonel Davis the ideal candidate for the position.

SUPERINTENDENT YEARS (1947-1965)

Now let us turn to the paper prepared by Colonel Davis that outlined his years as the Superintendent of the American Military Cemetery in Luxembourg City. The report by Colonel Davis highlights the magnitude of his job.

"The History of the Luxembourg American Military Cemetery Introduction"

As the time approaches when the management of this cemetery must change hands, it seems proper for the incumbent Superintendent to record in reasonable detail the textual and photographic history of the installation for the information of his successor. The period 1944-1965 is covered here. It is hoped that the successor, and his successors in turn, will have further occasion to add to this history as the years go by.

As of this writing, the history of the Luxembourg American Military Cemetery appears to embrace four periods, i.e.,

The Initial Burial Phase
The Repatriation of Remains Program
The Development of the Permanent Cemetery
The Subsequent years

The Initial Burial Phase
(December 1944 – March 1948)

In mid-December 1944, as Third Army units under General Patton's command became engaged in the Ardennes operation, the need for a burial terrain became immediately apparent. Third Army's G-4 toured the region and selected this site because it provided such essential features as a self-draining slope to a terrain free of heavy growth; good road connections; comparative isolation while still close to a community offering adequate labor, supply and railway facilities.

A service detachment was assigned at once to prepare the grounds. Prefabricated structures were erected among the bordering trees: an office, which stood about where the terrace plaque is at present; the garage section, located fifty yards behind the resent Plot C; a combined morgue and X-ray building near the present reservoir site. An ornamental fate near the actual northeast corner of Plot A was fabricated of rough-hewn birch trees and a sentry box was placed alongside. Primitive dirt roads interconnected these elements.

These facilities were not adequate for the administrative processing of the many remains brought here in the early phase of the counter-offensive. A staff of American and Luxembourg clerks was installed in the school building in Hamm to handle the records at this stage.

Burials were performed by labor troops, there being no mechanical equipment available. The bursting of German artillery shells fired from the

Moselle and Trier areas occasionally hampered work.

When communications allowed, grave markers of oak were tucked from the Belgian Ardennes. Painting and stenciling were done here.

By about March 1946, the burial program was completed (8,412 graves) and efforts were then directed toward improving the appearance of the grounds. Some 150 prisoners-of-war were rough there daily from the stockade in Howald and they performed such tasks as the construction of an attractive chapel and an office building containing a simple, but comfortable visitor's lounge.

American labor troops and German prisoners worked together to lay pathways among the (approximately) 24 rectangular plots existing at the time. For this single project, over nine hundred truckloads of coarse stone were hauled from the nearest source then in operation, a quarry near Esch-sur-Alzette.

On 12 April 1946, Mr. R. Warren Davis arrived on assignment from A.G.R.C. and became the first Superintendent of the cemetery. Officers and enlisted men were shifted progressively elsewhere, the POW's were also moved, and a local labor crew came into being.

During 1946-47, the main activities consisted of establishing lawns, planting flower beds, removing unneeded structures, improving roads and paths, and restoring those areas of the woods which had been damaged by military personnel and equipment.

The administrative staff continued to put all records in order, to establish grave locator files, and process numerous applications for grave adoption. The grave adoption program may have served some useful purpose, but human abuses were notable. In this community, for example, few asked to adopt a protestant or Jewish grave, none adopted an unknown. Moreover, the only graves to be adopted at all were those where's the "dog tag" on the marker also bore the deceased's home address. It is our opinion that the scheme should never have been encouraged.

The nearby German Military Cemetery, then comprising some 6-8,000 graves, was also placed under our responsibility, doubling the task of grounds maintenance and annual repainting of grave markers.

Unlike France, where the prior existence of World War I American cemeteries had established a modus operandi, Luxembourg was experiencing for the first time our non-combat activity and we were frequently hindered by officials who, while cordial, were unable to interpret existing regulations in our favor. Thus, we had literally to smuggle supplies – even paint for the grave markers – for a considerable period before reasonable importation arrangements could be worked out.

In 1947, the Superintendent was also charged with the temporary cemetery at Foy, near Bastogne, comprising 3,700 graves.

Visitor traffic in the years 1946-47 was impressive. On one particular Sunday, our guides actually counted some-what more than 14,600 persons entering the grounds.

As virtually every visitor wished to see General Patton's grave, it was impossible to maintain a lawn on the adjacent graves. By the end of a Sunday, visitors would have trod a rut six inches deep from the path to the grave, necessitating a re-sodding job in the morning. At our repeated urging, therefore, we were authorized to transfer the grave from a plot in the west end of the grounds to its present location. The transfer was affected on 19 March 1947.

Prior to the transfer, the authorities had wanted the grave to be moved to the west end of Row 1, Plot B. An unknown grave was placed at the east end of that row to establish architectural equilibrium. We maintained that this was no solution, however, as large touring groups insisted on being photographed around General Patton's cross, and the nearby graves would still be disturbed. The Plot B idea was thus abandoned, but this interim plan explains the presence of the unknown in Plot B, Row 1, Grave 2.

REPATRIATION OF REMAINS PROGAM
(March 1948 – December 1949)

In March1948, the cemetery was closed to visitors and screened with tarpaulins around its entire perimeter. Military personnel and morticians assembled, and 25 local laborers were hired to perform the exhumations.

A large hanger was erected in the East Meadow, site of the present garage, to which the remains were taken for final positive identification followed by casketing in massive, bronze-finished coffins. These containers weighed over 500 pounds, so that a narrow-gauge railway track was laid about the terrain to facilitate handling.

Processing of remains was interrupted briefly at times when phosphorous grenades still present in the remnants of a deceased's combat uniform burst into flame. All unexploded charges discovered at this stage were buried in a pit in the woods about 70 yards below, say, Grave 15 in the last row of Plot H.

From the processing hangar, the caskets were transported to a rented field in Hamm for storage under tarpaulins. Remains requested by N.O.K. for return to the United States were subsequently trucked to the port of Antwerp.

With all remains removed from the cemetery grounds, Contractor Emile Frank used bulldozers and sheepsfoot rollers to re-establish a true surface. Plans for the permanent arrangement of the graves area having been received, excavators dug continuous ditches along the proposed arcs, caskets were brought back from Hamm, laid in trenches with an accuracy of .01 foot with reference to established base marks, the earth replaced, graded and compacted.

Just prior to lowering, each remains received the interment rites of an appropriate clergyman. Cure Jacques Schmit of Hamm, Pastor Nicolas Housse of Luxembourg, and various Jewish Chaplains performed their services. The flag used in each case was mailed to the N.O.K.

It is to be noted for all the time that the remains were so carefully controlled during the entire period that an error in identification or in the location of any headstones is unthinkable. No visiting N.O.K. need ever entertain the slightest doubt in this regard.

It is also to be noted that, during this period, specialists examined some 267 unknown remains and positively identified all but 101 of them.

The exact figures are no longer at hand, but about 5,000 of our 8,412 remains were repatriated. A small temporary cemetery at Grand Failly, near Longwy, was closed out and we received a quota for interment here, brining our permanent total to 5,076. Thus, visitors who exclaim at the heavy battle toll reflected in the cemetery plots may be remained that a like number were returned home, so that the real toll was double the apparent one.

DEVELOPMENT OF THE PERMANENT CEMETERY
(December 1949 – July 1960)

Custody of the cemetery was transferred from A.G.R.C. to A.B.M.C. on 16 December 1949. Development of the grounds started promptly, following plans drawn by the New York firm of Voorhees, Walker, Foley and Smith.

It is an oddity that, while virtually the entire landscaping work was to be performed by contract, we ourselves, were left to clear the forest from the future terrace site. By selling the tree trunks to lumber dealers, we realized funds to purchase dynamite and equipment needed to remove the mass of tree stumps from the clearing.

The Superintendent transported the dynamite and explosive caps in his own car from the powder works at Kockekscheuer, making frequent trips with small quantities so that an explosion en route would not put too much of the community into orbit. As our laborers were reluctant to participate, Mr. John D. Mountjoy, the excellent Assistant Superintendent at that time, performed the placing and exploding of the charges almost single-handed. It was an arduous, dangerous undertaking, but only one casualty was recorded; a wildly soaring root severed the top third of one of our wooden flagpoles.

The so-called "Walker plans" envisioned a slab-roofed colonnade extending along the front edge of the terrace, with a glass-enclosed chapel nestling at the center point. As an influential member of the Commission objected adamantly to this conception, the original firm withdrew and was succeeded by

Architect Francis Keally of New York, and associates, who designed the existing structures on the basis of the predecessor's terrain arrangement, which we had already accomplished.

As a detailed description of these woks is given in our Guide's Talk pamphlet, we would mention here just a few interesting background incidents.

First, it is to be noted that the figure of the Angel on the chapel façade was carved in place, hewn in about four weeks' time by an elderly Italian sculptor and his two nephews. The block of New Orchid Red granite was so hard that chisels were blunted after every few strokes and it was necessary to lower them to the ground, where a field forges was operated continuously to dress the instruments.

Another interesting sidelight concerns the texts inscribed on the battle map pylons and the Walls of the Missing. These inscriptions were done in winter months and we had to enclose the sculptors' platform in plastic sheeting, with Butagaz heaters inside to warm both men and stone.

One-armed German sculptor carved a great proportion of these inscriptions. This man – a strong, cheerful individual in his early forties – had lost his right forearm on the Russian front. While in hospital, learning that his subsequent pension would have been greater if he had lost his arm above the elbow, he prevailed upon a complacent doctor to remove the injured arm near the shoulder. After demobilization, the man acquired a short leather sleeve affair, resembling a flowerpot with a small hammer stuck into the drain hole. Donning this contrivance at the work site and driving it with a lunge of his right shoulder, the man worked as swiftly and as accurately as did his colleagues, who, incidentally, worked in harmony with him despite their French nationality.

It may be mentioned in passing that the artisans who worked on the over-all project cam from England, Holland, Belgium, France, West-Germany, Italy and of course, Luxembourg.

During the construction period, Madame Perle Mesta, U.S. Minister, and His Excellency Mr. Joseph Bech, the Luxembourg Minister of Foreign Affairs, signed and Accord (20 March 1951) by which we received the use of the land in perpetuity. Outright title to the land had been offered, but this would have raised a problem of extra-territoriality, which was considered undesirable.

While we do not have any written evidence, it has always been our understanding that the Luxembourg authorities promulgated at that time a provision whereby no commercial ventures could be established within 500 meters of the cemetery. We do recall that one influential person was denied permission to construct a tourist hotel opposite the cemetery entrance, and the police have always assisted us in removing vendors from the parking area.

In that connection, we have long suspected that the terrain on the far side of the railroad line would eventually be subdivided into residential sections. We have nurtured trees for some years on our side of the line to insure the future privacy of our grounds on the west side.

The completed grounds and Memorial were dedicated on 4 July 1960 in a ceremony attended by Their Royal Highnesses the Grand Duchess Charlotte and the Prince of Luxembourg.

The Honorable Lyndon B. Johnson, then Vice-President of the United States, visited the cemetery on 4 November 1963.

Among other distinguished visitors received in the period 1944-65, the following may be mentioned:

Members of the Grand-Ducal Family
HRH Prince Jean, Hereditary Grand Duke
HRH Prince Charles
TRH the Princesses Marie-Adelaide, Marie-Gabrielle and Alix
The Honorable (later Sir) Winston S. Churchill
Miss Mary Churchill
Mr. Randolph L. Churchill

Mrs. Radolph L. Roosevelt

General Elliot Roosevelt

General Dwight D. Eisenhower

General George S. Patton, Jr.

Chancellor Figl of Austria

The Honorable Earl Warren
        Chief Justice of the Supreme Court
Le Marechel Juin

Prince Peter of Greece

Princess Charlotte de Ligne

Miss Margaret Truman
        Daughter of President Truman

Allowing for the repatriation period, during

which the cemetery was closed to the public, a close

and considered estimate – based partly on precise,

early records – would give the following total of

persons having visited these grounds as of 31

August 1965:

1944 –1948	400,000
1950 – 1964	2,205,000

Jan-Aug 1965   125,000
                 2,730,000

R. WARREN DAVIS
Superintendent

Reading of the Davis papers makes it clear that General Patton was the key attraction and it required moving his casket from the interior section to the front of the line and head of the column.

I visited the Cemetery on three separate occasions. The first in 1948 shortly after Colonel Davis became head of the Cemetery. During this trip, I helped separate the Army and Air Force installations based on the soon to be established United States Air Force.

My second visit was in 1962 while I was stationed at the NATO Defense College in Paris.

The third visit took place in 1998 and I was given the honor of laying a wreath on the Patton gravesite. It was a beautiful ceremony that was arranged under the supervision of Luxembourg officials (Figure 3-2).

Figure 3-2 Wreath laying ceremony

This photo shows my laying a wreath at the Patton gravesite. This colorful ceremony took place on October 4, 1998. I am in the center with my dear friend and colleague, LtCol Edwin Steinmeyer. Luxembourg dignitaries are also present.

From my visits and conversations with others, it is apparent that Patton's mystique is presently more pronounced than ever.

In 1985, my wife and I visited Arlington National Cemetery. We selected the site where we wised to be buried – on PATTON DRIVE (Exhibit 3-5) overlooking the Pentagon. Darlene, my wife of 50 years, died October 22,1992. Our headstone reads:

RICHARD JOSEPH STILLMAN

COLONEL

UNITED STATES ARMY

FEBRUARY 20, 1917 _____

WORLD WAR II

LEGION OF MERIT – BRONZE STAR

LUXEMBOURG ORDER OF THE CROWN

DEAREST WIFE AND MOTHER

DARLENE SLATER STILLMAN

OCTOBER 10, 1921 –OCTOBER 22, 1992

Figure 3-5 Stillman Burial Site on Patton Drive in Arlington National Cemetery

116

Now let us move from the three factual secret

missions to the two factious tales about my old boss.

PART FOUR
DID PATTON REALLY TALK TO GOD?

This section and the next separate fact and fiction. Patton followers are familiar with the Patton prayer delivered to all Third Army personnel in December 1944. But few have heard of the so-called conversation between "Old Blood and Guts" and God. Let us relate this fairy tale.

DID PATTON REALLY TALK TO GOD?

Surprise and consternation might best describe reaction of our Headquarters, Third Army staff on reading the following inscription:

"Lord, this is Patton speaking to You. These last two weeks were steps on our way to hell. Rain, snow, more rain and still more snow. I wonder, in vain, what's going on in Your Headquarters? On which side do You really stand? For three years now, my chaplains have maintained this war is a new Holy War, a new Crusade … the only difference being that the soldiers of this age take cover in tanks. They claim that we crossed the Atlantic to decidedly defeat the German armies and their atheistic Fuehrer so as to restore peace and liberty in Europe.

Until now I agreed with their statements because You gave us Your complete support. A splendid sea and a clear blue sky facilitated our landing in Africa and helped us to defeat Rommel, and the affair in Sicily was an expedition, which didn't amount to much. The weather was adequate for my tanks, in the accomplishment of what I would call the Greatest Victory You have granted to this day. You have guided me in the most grave decisions, even brining the Germans into traps, which facilitated my victory.

But now … exactly at the halfway mark, You bet on another horse … It seems to me that You put all Your assets in von Rundstedt's hands, as he, let's be honest, gives us much trouble.

My army is not trained or conditioned to endure a winter campaign. And You know that this climate is much more convenient for Eskimos than for the Southern States Riders whom I command …

Oh Lord, after reading this weather forecast I have come to the conclusion that either I or somebody else has offended You seriously, because I have to conclude that I have lost all of Your sympathies. It would be superfluous to add that our situation is desperate. Of course, I can go on telling my staff that all operations are developing as planned … But it is clear that my 101st Airborne

Division fighting in Bastogne is battling against the raging elements and that Gaffey, one of my best generals, suffers much more from the climate than from German attacks. I am not in the habit of lamenting, but my soldiers between Echternach and the Meuse are going through hell. I visited some hospitals and I saw terrible things, but the most terrible of all is that the total absence of visibility keeps my airplanes stuck on the ground. Thus, my flying artillery, without which I cannot fight, is useless. Even my reconnaissance planes cannot take off … and for 15 days I haven't been able to find out what's going on behind the German lines.

My God, it is impossible for me to fight in this gloom. Without Your help it will be impossible for me to study the enemy's tactics. Maybe You think I'm being unreasonable in talking to You, but I have lost all my patience with the chaplains who keep telling me that this atmospheric situation is typical Ardennes climate. To hell with faith and patience … You have to make up Your mind now! You have to help me so that on the occasion of Your Son's birthday I can offer Him the whole German Army as a Christmas present.

Lord, I am not unreasonable, I don't ask for impossible things. I don't want to perform a miracle. All I'm asking for is four days of "clear weather." Consent to give me as Your gift four days of blue sky, so my airplanes can take off, hunt, bomb, find their goals and annihilate them. Give me four days so that this mud can harden; allow my trucks to roll along and supply provisions and ammunition for my infantry, which needs it urgently. I need four whole days in order to send von Rundstedt and his army into the middle of Valhalla. It is too much of a burden for me to stand by powerless at the needless holocaust of our American youth. AMEN!"

We found this inscription on a plaque during our tour of Europe in October 1998. It was located in Luxembourg City at the entrance to Foundation Pescatore (Figure 4-1). This is the building the Third

Army Headquarters occupied for several months in the winter of 1944-45. It was the home for the aged prior to our arrival and reoccupied by the elderly on our departure. It is important to note that the chapel in the Foundation was used as a "War Room" during our stay there. It was restored to a chapel when we left.

Our visit to our old staff Headquarters building, as well as our entire stay in Luxembourg, was memorable.

We owe a hearty thank you to the men and women of CERCLE D'ETUDES sur la BATAILLE des ARDENNES. Note the outstanding program they arranged for us (Figure 4-2)

Figure 4-1 The Author at the Foundation Pescatore Entrance

Patton's "Conversation with God" plague is located at the entrance to the Foundation Pescature.

CERCLE D'ETUDES sur la BATAILLE des ARDENNES a.s.b.l.

GRAND-DUCHE DE LUXEMBOURG

IN THE FOOTSTEPS OF GENERAL PATTON

4 October 1998

8.30 Depart hotel
9.00 Hamm Cemetery wreathlaying at Gen. Patton's tomb
10.30 Visit Fondation Pescatore, former HQ 3rd Army
12.00 Lunch independant Luxembourg City
14.00 Depart Luxembourg City
15.00 Diekirch Historical Museum
16.30 Patton Monument Ettelbruck wreathlaying
17.00 Reception by the Mayor of Ettelbruck "Patton town"
18.00 Depart Ettelbruck

5 October 1998

8.30 Depart hotel
9.30 1944-1945 Liberation Memorial Carrefour Schuman
10.30 Bastogne Mardasson Monument and Historical Center
12.00 Lunch independant Bastogne
14.00 Depart Bastogne
15.00 GI Monument Clervaux wreathlaying
15.30 Reception at the castle
16.30 CEBA-Museum
17.00 Depart Clervaux
17.30 Vianden photo stop (castle)

Président:
Camille P. Kohn
1, rue Principale
L-7430 Fischbach

Vice-Président:
Jean Milmeister
1, rue de Brouch
L-7481 Tuntange

Secrétaire:
Mme Tilly Kinnen
20, rue de Huldsdorf
L-7324 Steinsel

Trésorier:
Jos. Schossert
9, rue du Village
L-6695 Winseler

Conservateur Musée:
Frank Rockar
Maison 158
L-9945 Aerzibom

Publiste:
Coldard Goergen
40, rue de Moutfort
L-5310 Contern

Bensable "Che Belge"
Henri Demeviller
rue de Reisenbourg

Figure 4-2 Program

126

In contrast to the secrecy surrounding Patton's so called "Conversation with God", the actual prayer is an open book and the facts are well known by our staff members. We recall the bitter cold days with its dark skies and heavy snow on the ground.

In view of the terrible weather, General Patton requested our head chaplain (Father James O'Neill), to ask the Lord to improve the weather elements. After reading the prayer and Christmas message, he ordered 360,000 copies be distributed to all individuals in the Third Army. The prayer and Christmas message were printed on 3x5 cards (Figure 4-3).

HEADQUARTERS
THIRD UNITED STATES ARMY

TO each officer and soldier in the Third United States Army, I wish a Merry Christmas. I have full confidence in your courage, devotion to duty, and skill in battle. We march in our might to complete victory. May God's blessing rest upon each of you on this Christmas Day.

G. S. PATTON, JR.,
Lieutenant General,
Commanding, Third United States Army

PRAYER

ALMIGHTY and most merciful Father, we humbly beseech Thee, of Thy great goodness, to restrain these immoderate rains with which we have had to contend. Grant us fair weather for Battle. Graciously hearken to us as soldiers who call upon Thee that armed with Thy power, we may advance from victory to victory, and crush the oppression and wickedness of our enemies, and establish Thy justice among men and nations. Amen.

Figure 4-3 Prayer and Christmas card

Now let us look at the military situation and why Patton deemed the prayer so important.

This phase of combat for the Third Army was officially referred to as the "Bastogne – St. Vith Campaign (December 19, 1944 – January 28, 1945). It was, however; better know as the "Battle of the Bulge." I was out daily in the combat zone observing the military situation and reporting my findings to Bradley and Patton's headquarters.

By mid-December 1944, the weather had turned bitter cold. Third Army had its forces east along the Moselle River. The First U.S. Army and the British and Canadian forces were also facing to the east preparatory to launching a coordinated attack. This all changed beginning at 5:30 a.m., December 16, when a Nazi Army Group, spearheaded by Panzer tank and motorized Infantry units, under Field Marshal Gerd von Rundstedt smashed through lightly guarded American forces in the Ardennes. Thus began what became known as the Battle of the Bulge.

As the map indicates (Figure 4-4), the Germans attacked on three fronts, crossing northern Luxembourg on the southern flank and moving into Belgium with two other forces. These Nazi Panzer divisions were the cream of the German troops. They struck in an area that was thought to be impassable, much like what occurred in World War I when they attacked the same area. This time they did it with such secrecy that the Allies had no warning. The success of their surprise tactics was due in part to the fact that the weather was so bad (fog, rain, snow) that Allied air power was virtually immobilized and no reconnaissance missions could be flown.

Rundstedt's surprise counteroffensive was initially very successful. His three armies opened a 45-mile-wide front in the First U.S. Army sector. Its deepest penetration was 60 miles. This breakthrough split General Bradley's command when he lost contact with Hodge's badly mauled First Army and left him with only Third Army as Eisenhower gave Montgomery temporary command of Hodge's troops. The Nazi objective was the important port at Antwerp, Belgium. With this prize, Rundstedt would have completely divided the Allied forces and prevented much needed supplies from reaching them.

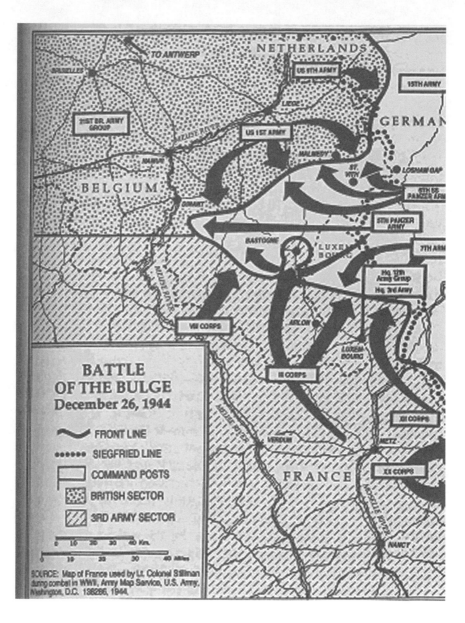

Figure 4-4 Battle of the Bulge

The initial Rundstedt success was apparent to me upon observing the disorganization of U.S. troops on the southern flank of the counterattack. I spoke with Lt. General Troy Middleton (VIII Corps Commander) at a crossroads in northern Luxembourg. He was directing traffic as remnants of his units escaped to regroup. Middleton had no knowledge of the Rundstedt troop locations as his communication net was completely cut off. There was utter confusion and the rumor spread that German soldiers dressed in American uniforms planned to kill high-ranking U.S. commanders.

The Nazis did parachute several dozen English-speaking soldiers dressed in American uniforms in an effort to create panic in our rear areas. They were volunteers who had been trained by Lt.

Colonel Otto Skorzeny, the same person who had rescued Benito Mussolini after his imprisonment in Italy. Skorzeny also was reported to have had a team planning to kill Eisenhower. To counter this effort, our Military Police and others were stationed at intersections and key military installations. The security worked – all the enemy soldiers were captured.

Within three days after the initial Nazi attack, Eisenhower recognized that this was a major offensive. He called a meeting, at Bradley's Headquarters, of all his senior officers.   Gloom and doom, I observed, pervaded the large briefing room. G-2 presented the current situation and the impact of the German breakthrough. Eisenhower then outlined his counterattack. He asked Patton when he would be ready to attack. Patton replied, "December 22nd with three divisions." Prior to leaving Third Army Headquarters, Patton instructed his staff to proceed with planning for the relocation of his troops.

The repositioning of the Third Army troops, in spite of the bitter cold weather, was accomplished with great efficiency. In large measure, the success was due to the improved weather conditions that enabled our air power to provide continuous bombing missions.

The Patton prayer and the Christmas message proved to be great morale builders and were warmly received by the troops. I noted that the size of the card was ideal for inclusion in a wallet. Some carried it for many years as a good luck memento.

CONCLUSION

The authentic Patton prayer reflected Patton's true belief in the Lord. He was a devoutly religious man and attended church each Sunday and read his bible daily. He kept a copy by his bedside, and was a truly a loyal Episcopalian. From personal observations and conversations with the General, it is so obvious he would never have had the so-called "Conversation with God." The entire tone of the fictitious talk is so truly "unpatton", that it is laughable. Unfortunately either unknowingly or intentionally some people have picked it up for real.

PART FIVE

WHEN (AND HOW) DID PATTON POSSESS THE SPEAR OF LONGINUS?

This final section provides information on the history of the Longinus Spear. I found it made for good reading. However, in regards to the Patton connection it has no basis in fact.

Informed of Patton and the Spear

The second factious, Patton story relates to the Spear of Longinus. Here is how I came into the picture. In recent years, I have appeared frequently on the Keith Rush radio show (WASO, New Orleans, LA). He is a highly respected radio personality with over 50 years of broadcasting experience.

During a 2001 appearance on his show, I received a call from a listener, Glenn Ferrand. He inquired if I was familiar with the tale about Patton and the Spear of Longinus. I replied; "No." A few days later he sent me the following letter:

"Dear Dr. Stillman:

I'm the person who called the Keith Rush show to ask you if you knew information regarding "The Spear of Longinus".

Since you said that you did not, I found some references to it on the Internet and printed it to send to you.

I do not believe everything I read on the Internet, but I had heard about "The Spear of Longinus" years before the Internet was invented.

The reference to General Patton is listed on page 3, paragraph 3. There seems to be some credible evidence that the story may be true.

Sincerely,
Glenn Ferrand"

I replied to Glenn the next day:

"Glenn – how thoughtful to send me the information on the "Spear" and so promptly – Thank you. A colleague at the University of New Orleans listened to Keith and brought me two items on the Spear from the Internet. I checked several authorities on GSP and they all agree that someone had a vivid imagination. Richard"

The item on the Internet that Glenn referred to

stated:

"From that point on, history of this lance becomes quite specific. An Army officer took possession of the lance in the name of the U.S. Government on April 30,1945. With the exception of General George Patton, Commander of the U.S. Third Army, American generals and political leaders showed little interest in the spear. Patton, on the other hand, was terribly interested in it and had its history traced and its authenticity confirmed. After a time, General Eisenhower had the spear returned to the Hofburg Treasure House, where it remains.[4]"

A second print out of four pages appeared on the Internet and is entitled "Hitler and the Italy Lance." It was written by Bill Kolagunis and dated 9/25/01. The following are the paragraphs that pertain to my old boss.

---

[4] Source: From the Internet printout. Page 3 of 5 page entitled "The Spear of Longinus.

"As aside to this story about Hitler and the Lance is the fact there is another story about General George S. Patton of the United States Army. In light of the Spear's incredible legend, Patton is said to have become extremely upset at General Eisenhower's decision to return such a great talisman of power of Hapsburgs. Consequently, some people have theorized that the lance which was actually returned to Vienna may not have been the original spearhead, but that it is, rather, a copy – a counterfeit –of the original which Patton insisted be retained by the United States.

Whether or not the lance, which currently resides in Vienna is the *original* one which Hitler stole, or whether it's only a counterfeit, one thing is certain: And that is that George Patton was not only one of the greatest generals in the history of warfare, having taken more land and killed more enemy soldiers, and taken more prisoners than any other general in history, he was also one of the world's greatest mystics as well.

Twentieth Century Fox's great classic motion picture of 1970, which won 8 Academy Awards including Best Picture that year, ***Patton***, told the story of a man who was so mystical in his belief about his own personal destiny as a soldier that the movie quite rightly underscored a number of places Patton's belief in reincarnation in which he stated that he had lived many previous lives in countless ages of the past, always as a great warrior.

And if Patton could have seriously believed such incredible mystical ideas, then it is certainly possible that he might have used his power to secure what he believed to be such a potential great talisman of power as the Holy Lance for his *own* country, orders not withstanding."

Story of the Spear

I agree with Mr. Kolagunis on the accomplishments of General Patton, but find no facts to support the lance material. Now let us comment on the Spear of Longinus.

A mention of the Spear appears in the bible:

"John 19:34 …But one of the soldiers with a spear pierced his side, and forthwith came there out blood and water"[5]

The soldier who thrust the spear into the side of Jesus was named Longinus – a member of the Roman Legion. Thus, the spear became known as the "Spear of Longinus". In the centuries that followed after the crucifixion of Christ, the Spear took on a mystical quality.

---

[5] King James Version -

Leading military/political figures like Charlemagne, believed that carrying the Spear gave them supernatural powers. Prior to World War II, the Spear (also known as the Holy Lance) resided in a Museum in Vienna, Austria. When Hitler occupied Austria he took possession of the Spear and sent it to Germany. Here it remained until U.S. Forces discovered it and returned the Spear to the Vienna Museum.

In order to find further information on the Spear, I contacted Mr. Philip Lorio, on July 2, 2003. He is an attorney located in New Orleans and the Honorary Consul General to the Republic of Austria. He kindly sent me a fax the following day that said:

"Per our conversation, please find the page from the Green Michelin Guide to Austria which discusses the "holy lance". I did a quick search on the Internet and there are many, many entries on the Spear of Longinus. Good luck and all my best. Phil Lorio"

The Green Michelin Guide to Austria refers to the "holy lance" that is kept in a Museum in Vienna.

144

Based on information from Mr. Lorio, I contacted the Curator from Vienna:

"Dear Curator:

The purpose of this email is to determine if you have information on the Spear of Longinus in regards to the following matters:

- History of the Spear
- Photos of the Spear
- Location of the Spear
- Connection of Gen. George S. Patton, Jr. to the Spear.

I am a Professor Emeritus at the University of New Orleans (New Orleans, Louisiana, USA). During WWII, I was an aide to General Patton and saw him daily on the battlefield in Europe. I am presently writing my third book on the General (General Patton's Secret Missions: Little Know Facts about intriguing Experiences of 'Old Blood and Guts').

Kindly inform me of any cost for the photos and other information.

I look forward with pleasure to hearing from you,

Richard J. Stillman, Ph.D.
Colonel, U.S. Army Retired"

I received the following reply from Dr. Franz Kirchweger, Curator at the Kunsthistorisches Museum. It reads in part:

"The object you are interested in is the Holy Lance which is kept in the collections of the Kunsthistorisches Museum Wein (Ecclesisatical Treasury). A Hofburg Museum – as mentioned in your email – does not exist. You can find an image of the object on our website (www.khm.at). Modern scholars have found out that this object, which was thought to be the Spear of Longinus for centuries, is in fact a Carolingian lance and thus dates back only to the 8th century. The history of the Spear of Longinus is actually very complicated (changing its attributions – to Constantine, Longinus, St. Maurice – several times in history). The lance was brought to Nuremberg in 1939, where it stayed until 1945. Then it was brought back to Vienna. According to our knowledge there is no evidence, that General Patton was especially interested or personally involved in the return of the insignia and relics of the Holy Roman Empire (where the lance is only one item among many important objects) to Austria. We know that there exist a lot of strange theories, creating a "Spear of Destiny", in

146

American books (i.e. Ravenscroft). If you read Ernst Kubin – Muchen 1991 – you will find a careful research on this subject, making definitely clear that Ravenscroft invented a lot of nonsense.

There are B&W photographs of the Viennes lance. If you should need colour-transparentcies or information on the costs (photographs, reproductions fees etc.), I have to ask you, to get in touch with our department for reproduction rights, Mrs. lise Jung. They will be happy, to help you with more information.

Thank you for your interest in the collections of the Kunsthistorisches Museum Wien.

Sincerely Yours

Dr. Franz Kirchweger

Curator"

As noted above, the Curator pointed out that much had been written about the lance and, to include, Patton's connection to it. He confirmed my belief that Patton had no relationship with the Spear of Longinus. I liked his term; "Nonsense" and so informed him.

In addition to the material from Dr. Franz Kirchweger, I received helpful information from the Vienna Museum that includes the following description of the Spear:

> The Holy Lance (Figure 5-1) is a Carolingian winged lance with perforated work of unequalled perfection: a pointed, oval aperture chiseled out of the center of the blade with a forged ornamental iron pins inserted into it. At the lower end of the lance are two blades that were added later and that extend to the wings of the lance and are tied to it with narrow thongs.
>
> The first known description of the Holy Lance is found in the History of Luitprand of Cremona, which he completed in 961. Luitprands description of the Holy Lance is consistent with the actual data. The Holy Lance does indeed have crosses inlaid in brass on the knots of the pin as well as on the wings of the lance. Tiny reliquary particles of the nails of the

Cross-have been forged into the lance in the shape of a cross for identification.

Luitprand says noting about the reliquary character of the Holy Lance, but gives an account of its history, according to which in 921/22, Count Samson and his partisans entrusted dominion over the regnum Italicum, to Rudolf, king of Burgundy, along with the Holy Lance, begging him to drive to drive out Emperor Berengar. However, since the reliquary lance was a "treasure by which God binds the earthly and celestial, the German king Henry secured its possession by bestowing lavish gifts on the Burgundian king. A tradition must have developed over the centuries obviously determined by the wishful thinking of the lance's owner whereby the particles of various nails of the Cross - became the one - clavus domini that the iron pin was held to be, as it was mentioned in the inscription on the silver band of Emperor Henry IV

(Ruled 1084-1105). It remains unclear why the point of the lance was renamed St. Maurice in the inscription in which the Holy Lance is expressly addressed as a dual relic. It is also unclear whether the weapon served as a Franconian or Langobardian lance of power following the Carolingian era.

The Holy Lance remained the noblest imperial insignia for a long time, but its aura merged with that of the second imperial relic, the Particle of the Cross, during the Salian era. In later years there were intentions to increase the nimbus of the Holy Lance by reinterpreting it as the Lance of Longinus. In the first third of the 13th century, a papal document mentions the Holy Lance for the first time as a dual Passion relic, but only in the 14th century was its interpretation as a lance of Passion officially accepted.

Emperor Charles IV ordered the inscription naming it the "Lance and the Nail of the Lord" around 1354 on the

golden   sleeve   visible   today   and
introduced the Feast of the Holy Lance."

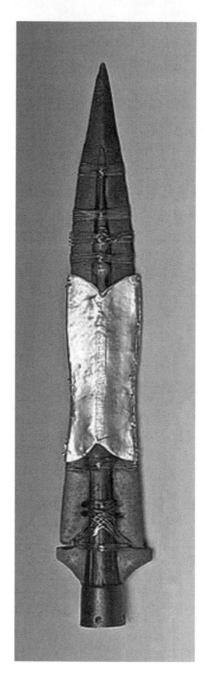

Figure 5-1 Spear of Longinus

CONCLUSION

This background on the Spear (the Lance) would have been of interest to General Patton. Furthermore, the Lance was recovered from the Nazis in an area that was taken by our Third Army troops.

The evidence, however, supports the fact that my boss was **not** ever involved with any aspect of the Lance.

Patton never mentioned the Spear in either my conversations with him or in his writing. Furthermore, there was nothing in our Third Army files referring to the Spear and none of my Third Army colleagues from World War II who served on Patton's staff ever spoke of the Spear.

In summary, the Lance that would have been of interest to Patton is located at the

Kunsthistorisches Museum in Vienna, Austria.

General Patton, in my view, had no

connections with the Spear of Longinus.

A PARTING THOUGHT

The findings from research, writings and

recollections of my old boss confirm that the first

three secret missions (Fortitude; Huntington Library;

Luxemburg Cemetery) are factual.

In contrast the last two stories are fictitious.

I would like to take this opportunity to thank you

for reading my book and welcome your comments.

APPENDIX A

BRIEF BIOGRAPHY
GENERAL GEORGE S. PATTON, JR.

George Smith Patton, Jr. was born at Lake Vineyard Ranch (near San Gabriel, California) on November 11, 1885. He was appointed to the United States Military Academy from California in 1904. Academic difficulties resulted in his spending an extra year at West Point. He was commissioned a Second Lieutenant of Calvary on June 11, 1909.

Other highlights included:

❖ Set an Academy high hurdles record (1908).

❖ Married Beatrice Banning Ayer (1910).[6]

❖ Finished fifth in the Olympic Military Pentathlon in Stockholm, Sweden (1912). Events included

---

[6] The couple had three children: Beatrice, Ellen and George. The son was named George Smith Patton IV. General George Smith Patton, Jr. was the grandson of the first Patton to carry the name. GSP Jr.'s father was christened George William Patton, but at the age of 11, he asked his parents to change his name to George Smith Patton in honor of his father. Nevertheless, his son, the famous General, was named George Smith Patton, Jr. GSP, Jr. wanted to set the chronology record straight and named his son George Smith Patton IV. There is presently a grandson of GSP, Jr. named George Smith Patton V.

cross-country run, fencing, pistol shooting, steeplechase and swimming.

❖ Participated in the Punitive Expedition in Mexico as General Pershing's aide (1916-17).

❖ Rose through the ranks from Second Lieutenant to Colonel (between 1909 and 1918).

❖ Sailed for France in May 1917, as a member of General Pershing's staff.

❖ Assigned to Tank Service at his request (1917).

❖ Observer at Cambrai when tanks were first used on a large scale by the British. Commander, Light Tank Center and later several tank units including 30thtank Brigade. Wounded during the Meuse Argonne offensive (1918).

❖ Received the Purple Heart and Distinguished Service Cross (1918).

❖ Reduced in rank to Captain (1920) for one day[7]

---

[7] The Official Army Register does not indicate that Patton was reduced in rank from Colonel to Captain. It was only for a day, but he remained a Major for nearly 14 years. I saw my friends and colleagues reduced one rank after World War II, and it was a bitter pill to swallow. A former boss of mine in the War Department was dropped two grades, Major General to Colonel.

- ❖ Promoted to Brigadier General in 1940 and to Major General in 1941.

- ❖ Landed with United States troops in North Africa on November8, 1942, and commanded II Corps in Tunisia.

- ❖ Promoted to Lt. General on March 12, 1943.

- ❖ Commanded the Seventh Army in Sicily, Third Army in Europe and the Fifteenth Army in American-occupied Germany.

- ❖ Promoted to General April 14, 1945.

- ❖ His decorations from the U.S. Government during World Wars and II include the Distinguished Service Cross with Oak Leaf Cluster, the Distinguished Service Medal with Two Oak Leaf Clusters, the Legion of Merit, the Silver Star and Purple Heart. He also received numerous foreign decorations.

- ❖ General Patton died in a U.S. military hospital in Heidelberg, Germany, on December 21, 1945, as a result of automobile accident. He was buried three days later in the American Military Cemetery in Luxembourg.

APPENDIX B

THE LIFE AND TIMES OF
GENERAL GEORGE S. PATTON, JR
1885-1945
STILLMAN'S LIFE SPAN CHART AND A
BRIEF BIOGRAPHY

This chart about George Patton is a miniature on the one I created and published in 1990. It depicts the life and time of General George S. Patton, Jr. (1885-1945) as well as a graphic history of key happenings during his life. The three-color poster lists significant political, military, technological and economic events between 1885-1945. Also included are Patton quotes, photos, and his leadership principles based on my personal observations. I was a member of Patton's Third Army staff (Lucky Forward) during World War II. At the end of the war, I became Secretary General Staff with an office next to the General.

To obtain a copy of my Patton chart, complete and mail the form on the following page.

Please send me _____copies of Stillman's Patton chart at $40.00 each plus $5.00 for shipping and handling. For shipments outside the U.S. add $5.00 (for air mail shipment, add $20.00). Quotes available on quantity orders (10 or more) Make checks payable in U.S. DOLLARS DRAWN ON A U.S. BANK.

I am enclosing the amount of $ _____

Money Order _____Check_____

Make money orders or checks payable to Dr. R. J. Stillman.

Mail to Dr. R. J. Stillman, Lake Oaks, 2311 Oriole Street, New Orleans, LA 70122.*

 * Inquiries, call R. J. Stillman Co. at (504) 288-8112

NAME: _____

ADDRESS: _____

CITY _____STATE: _____ ZIP: _____

Professor Stillman is also publisher and creator of the best seller chart entitled DOW JONES INDUSTRIAL AVERAGE: 1896-PRESENT (36"x24") (with Stillman's Significant Political, Military, Technological and Economic Events), $40.00 for current edition plus $5.00 for shipping and handling, and SUPER BOWLS & DOW INDUSTRIALS (18"x24") (with Stillman's Comparative History and Young Predications), $20.00 plus $5.00 for shipping and handling.

160

APPENDIX C

CORPS AND DIVISIONS UNDER PATTON'S COMMAND

CORPS

III CORPS	VIII COPRS	XV CORPS
V CORPS	XIII CORPS	XX CORPS

DIVISIONS

1st Infantry Division	4th Armored Division	76th Infantry Division
2nd Infantry Division	5th Armored Division	79th Infantry Division
4th Infantry Division	6th Armored Division	80th Infantry Division
5th Infantry Division	7th Armored Division	83rd Infantry Division
8th Infantry Division	8th Armored Division	86th Infantry Division
26th Infantry Division	9th Armored Division	87th Infantry Division
28th Infantry Division	10th Armored Division	89th Infantry Division
29th Infantry Division	11th Armored Division	90th Infantry Division
35th Infantry Division	12th Armored Division	94th Infantry Division
42nd Infantry Division	13th Armored Division	95th Infantry Division
65th Infantry Division	14th Armored Division	97th Infantry Division
70th Infantry Division	16th Armored Division	99th Infantry Division
71st Infantry Division	20th Armored Division	2nd French Armored Division
	17th Airborne Division	
	101st Airborne Division	

APPENDIX D

HEADQUARTERS THIRD U.S ARMY STAFF (SECTION CHIEFS)

The following is the official published list of section chiefs of Patton's Headquarters, Third U.S. Army, as of September 24, 1945. At the time this was published, my office was next door to General Patton's at Bad Tolz, Germany.

Chief of Staff (Actg)	Colonel Paul D. Harkins	017625	GSC
Deputy C/S (Actg)	Colonel Charles L. Heitman, Jr.	018059	FA
AC of S, G-1	Colonel Frederick S. Matthews	05625	GSC
AC of S, G-2 (Actg)	LtCol Edward J. Schmuck	0349795	GSC
AC of S, G-3	Brig Gen Halley G. Maddox	012852	GSC
AC of S, G-4 (Actg)	Colonel William H. Harrison	0292346	GSC
AC of S, G-5	Colonel Roy L. Dalferes	010279	GSC
Secretary General Staff	Colonel Richard J. Stillman	025038	GSC
Adjutant General (Actg)	Colonel Lorraine L. Manly	0300272	AGD
Antiaircraft Officer	Colonel Frederick R. Chamberlain	010585	CAC
Army Exchange Section	Colonel Richard Sears	014801	FA
Artillery Officer	Brig Gen Edward J. Williams	012818	FA
Chaplain	Colonel James J. O'Neill	016370	Ch C
Chemical Warfare Officer	Colonel George J. B. Fisher	08257	CWS
Claims Section	Colonel Henry B. Curtis	0125355	FA
Engineer Officer (Actg)	Colonel Donald A. Elliget	019719	CE
Finance Officer	Colonel Charles B. Milliken	020340	FD
Hq Comdt & CO Sp Trs	Colonel Thomas M. Brinkley	012189	INF
Information Control	Colonel B.B. McMahon	07040	IGD
Judge Advocate	Colonel Charles C. Park	07176	JAGD
Ordnance Officer	Colonel Thomas R. Taber	09775	ORD
Provost Marshall	Colonel Philip C. Clayton	05210	CAV
Public Relations Officer	Major Ernest Deane	0412496	GMC
Quartermaster	Colonel Everett Busch	07260	QMC

Signal Officer	Colonel Elton F. Hammond	012291	SIG C
Special Service Officer	LtCol C. L. Hail	017779	INF
Surgeon	Colonel Thomas J. Hartford	018330	MC
Transportation Officer	Colonel Light B. Yost	0288323	TC

SIGNATURE OF GENERALPATTONAND KEY STFF MEMBERS, OFFICE OF THE COMMANDING GENERAL

G.S. PATTON, JR.
General

VAN S. MERLE-SMITH, JR.
Major, FA
Aide –de-Camp

PAUL D. HARKINS
Colonel, GSC
Actg Chief of Staff

RIHARD J. STILLMAN
LtCol, GSC
Secretary General Staff

CHARLES L.HEITMAN, JR.
Colonel, FA
Actg Deputy Chief of Staff

ROY B. MAURER
Capt., NMB,
Asst. Secy. Gen. Staff

F. P. GRAVES, JR.
CATAIN, FA
Aide-de-Camp

APPENDIX E

OFFICERS HEADQUARTERS THIRD
ARMY STAFF

All officers who were members of General Patton's Third Army Staff are extremely proud of this experience. Here is the official list as it appeared in the **Army Action Report Third U.S. Army 1 August 1944 – 9 May 1945.** It includes all officers assigned to Headquarters. Third Army during the period covered by this report. It also lists all officers attached to the Headquarters for at least six months during the period August 1, 1944 – May 9, 1945.

A study of this list highlights the wide range of activities required to manage an organization of 250,000 to 400,000 people. Leaders who run cities this size have their share of problems. Add to these problems a city that is constantly relocating and sustaining combat casualties. It also must be fed, clothed, housed and provided medical attention.

COMMANDING GENERAL AND AIDES

Gen	Patton, G. S. Jr.	O 2605	USA
LtCol	Codman, Charles R.	O 448161	MI
Maj	Stiller, Alexander C.	O 1010000	ADC
Capt	Graves, Francis P. Jr.	O 439195	FA

CHIEF OF STAFF SECTION

Maj Gen	Gaffey, Hugh J.	O 8435	GSC
Maj Gen	Gay, Hobart R.	O 7323	GSC
Col	Harkins, Paul D.	O 17625	GSC
Maj	Murnane, George F. Jr.	O 1010331	CAV
Capt	Taylor, Elliott R.	O 379074	CAV
Capt	Wysong, Alison C. Jr.	O 453526	INF

SECRETARY TO GENERAL STAFF

LtCol	Pfann, George R.	O 469770	GSC
Capt	Maurer, Rov B.	O2053898	AUS
CWO	Buels, Monroe T.	W 2108647	NMB

G-1 SECTION

Col	Matthews, Frederick S.	O 5625	GSC
Col	Horne, William A. Jr.	O 296185	GSC
LtCol	Foote, Thomas C.	O 19488	FA
LtCol	Thomas, T. K.	O 364492	GSC
LtCol	Wing, Robert B.	O 275785	CAV
LtCol	Pelton, Joseph A.	O 329346	GSC
LtCol	Eklund, Coy G.	O 379547	CAV
Maj	La Rue, Robert G.	O 216396	INF
Maj	Rentro, Forney Jr.	O 313676	FA
Maj	Richardson, Hugh F.	O 461042	INF
Capt	Hess, Buie	O 1002647	AGD
Capt	Veitenthal, Carl E. Jr.	O 1003060	AGD
1stLt	Cassell, Ray E.	O 1312123	INF
CWO	Miller, Richard F.	W 2108639	NMB

G-2 SECTION

Col	Koch, Oscar W.	O 10851	GSC
Col	Allen, Robert S.	O 481033	GSC
LtCol	Carter, Bernard S.	O 885628	GSC
LtCol	Franklin, Horace A.	O 221725	GSC
LtCol	Schmuck, Edward J.	O 349795	AGD
LtCol	Huot, Louis C.	O 914204	INF
Maj	Popovsky, Nicholas T.	O 275566	AC
Maj	Cheadle, John F.	O 353837	FA
Maj	Swanson, George D.	O 329738	CAV
Maj	Ordway, Howard E.	O 342012	INF
Maj	Rose, Edward A.	O 885076	AUS
Capt	Twelmeyer, Theodore A.	O 355058	CAV
Capt	Du Bose, Horace M. Jr.	O 506094	MI
Capt	Newman, John A.	O325448	CE
Capt	Robinson, James J.	O 885436	INF
Capt	Goolrick, William K. Jr.	O 438144	INF
Capt	Benson, Walter L.	O 394619	CAV
Capt	Dieter, John P.	O 1030357	CAV
Capt	Krister, Tom M.	O 479170	CAV
Capt	Dimmier, George F.	O 1040911	CAC
1stLt	Katz, Abraham A.	O 912666	ORD
1stLt	Wilson, Neal B.	O 1320267	INF
2ndLt	Grosso, Louis J.	O 1946972	TC
2ndLt	Law, Howard A. Jr.	O 885668	INF
WOJG	Hose, Fred H.	W 2121157	NMB

G-2 AIR

Col	Forde, Harold M.	O 16409	GSC
LtCol	McIntosh, Kenneth	O 204150	INF
LtCol	Pajerski, Frank J.	O 385905	CE
Maj	Scheerer, Theodore J.	O 258891	INF
Maj	Bigger, Chester H.	O 24212	FA
Maj	Clark, James C.	O 409383	FA
Maj	Patterson, Dallas M.	O 408938	INF
Capt	Reiner, Lawrence J.	O 370014	INF
Capt	Mershon, Carroll M.	O 391959	FA

Capt	Scott, Gordon W.	O 303546	CAV
Capt	Eastham, William K.	O 1042278	CAC
Capt	Foltz, Albert B.	O 293514	INF
Capt	Gilliam, Richard C.	O 316749	INF
Capt	Campbell, William R.	O 345074	INF
Capt	Clark, James F.	O 449745	INF
1stLt	Moncure, Thomas R.	O 408203	INF
1stLt	Barlow, Lester	O 1298486	INF
1stLt	Levy, Jerome K.	O 1285445	INF
1stLt	Marchus, David E.	O 1284356	INF

ATTACHED
COUNTER INTELIGENCE CORPS

Capt	Hallett, James B.	O 1304523	INF
Capt	Callen, Albert S.	O 1305891	INF
Capt	Ray, James E.	O 1031121	CAV
Capt	Sayers, Sam R. Jr.	O 1320567	INF
1stLt	Yarnevich, Ernest N.	O 1318392	INF
2ndLt	Oliver, Paul E.	O 1998023	AUS
2ndLt	Burglund, Oliver O.	O 1997991	AUS
2ndLt	Cody, Charles J.	O 2000155	AUS
2ndLt	Coyne, Martin J.	O 1997990	AUS
2ndLt	Vaivada, Anthony S.	O 2001159	AUS
2ndLt	Fanning, Julius N. Jr.	O 2001133	AUS

ENEMY DOCUMENT SECTION

Capt	Pressler, John I.	O 1109599	CE
2ndLt	Stein, Joseph	O 2015831	AUS

FIELD INTERROGATION DETACHMENT

Maj	Marechal, Hans H.	O 129146	INF
Capt	Van Dam, Bernard E.	O 1298789	INF

MILITARY INTELLIGENCE INTERPRETER TEAMS

Capt	Wege, Hans F.	O 275181	SIG C
1stLt	Thompson, Cyril S.	O 1311705	INF
1stLt	Onffroy, Paul D.	O 1053289	CAC

OFFICE OF STRATEGIC SERVICES DETACHMENT

LtCol	Shallcross, Lawrence B.	O 298590	CAV
Maj	Haensel, Andrew	O 444029	SN C
Capt	Barnes, Charles de M.	O 1284450	INF
Capt	Tarrant, Warren J.	O 1004527	AGD
1stLt	Moller, Mogens P.	O 1299451	INF
1stLt	Mueller, Gustave A.	O 1593973	QMC
1stLt	Perry, John S.	O 886330	AUS

ORDER OF BATTLE UNIT

Capt	Gerber, Helmut E.	O 1599850	QMC

PHOTO INTERPRETATION TEAMS

Capt	Chalif, Edward L.	O 1305726	INF
Capt	Knight, Franklin Jr.	O 1171633	FA
Capt	Ward, Maurice A.	O 1583813	ORD
Capt	Snow, Richard S.	O 1040128	CAC
Capt	Cicero, Raymond F.	O 1302602	INF
Capt	Martin, Evans J.	O 1043159	CAC
1stLt	Morus, Henry	O 1317989	INF
1stLt	Pisano, Joseph F.	O 1323352	INF
1stLt	Schappich, Leon N.	O 1049334	CAC
1stLt	Macon, Boise	O 526757	CAC
1stLt	Sporic, Stephen	O 1037919	CAC
1stLt	OLear, Mike	O 10336833	CAC
1stLt	Wright, Albert S.	O 361669	CAC
1stLt	Wruble, Harvey M.	O 1059689	CAC

PRISONER OF WAR INTERROGATION TEAMS

Capt	Kovach, Frank Z.	O 407698	CAV
Capt	Neumann, Fred S.	O 1179985	FA
1stLt	Jann, Edmund C.	O 1317088	INF
1stLt	Lang, Herman L.	O 1326099	INF
2ndLt	Goldschmidt, Lucien C.	O 2015942	AUS
2ndLt	Sheridan, Henry	O 2011941	AUS
2ndLt	Wallach, Ernest	O 2015941	AUS
2ndLt	Heilbrunn, Martin	O 2015969	AUS

PSYCHOLOGICAL WARFARE BRANCH

1stLt	Collette, Jack T.	O 437097	CAV
2ndLt	Littman, Edward H.	O 2010514	AUS
2ndLt	Nilson, Nils C.	O 2010513	AUS

SPECIAL LIAISON UNIT

1stLt	Hull, Lawrence C.	O 1821872	CAV
1stLt	Brown, William N.	O 2041083	INF

G-3 SECTION

Brig Gen	Maddox, Halley G.	O 12852	GSC
Col	Wallace, Brenton G.	O 185391	FA
Col	Hensey, Walter R. Jr.	O 14950	FA
Col	Griffin, William E.	O 11894	CAC
Col	Borders, William A.	O 222335	GSC
LtCol	Goodwin, James E.	O 201158	FA
LtCol	Wright, Joseph H.	O 267842	GSC
LtCol	Keehn, Roy D. Jr.	O 246642	CAV
LtCol	Stillman, Richard J.	O 25038	INF
LtCol	Hanson, Ruben N.	O 235903	FA
LtCol	Hoover, Richard S.	O 270135	GSC
LtCol	Pester, Eugene W.	O 338294	INF
LtCol	Dugan, Harold M.	O 289317	INF
LtCol	Doerr, Paul L.	O 247717	INF

LtCol	Leeney, Lewis W.	O 25206	INF
Maj	Lindau, Fred I.	O 225962	CE
Maj	Sutton, Alexander G. Jr.	O 328595	CE
Maj	Paynter, Charles A.	O 322898	INF
Maj	Shirley, John E.	O 352763	CAC
Maj	Bredin, Ryerson, A.	O 297346	ORD
Maj	Davis, John M.	O 314057	CAV
Maj	Hilliard, Lee H.	O 404242	INF
Maj	Wolf, John F.	O 373131	INF
Maj	James, Ernest J.	O 241849	CE
Maj	Helbig, Herbert R. Jr.	O 379956	FA
Maj	Holton, Ira J.	O 453734	INF
Maj	Stinemeyer, Edwin H. Jr.	O 270546	CE
Maj	Gundlach, Robert L.	O 430533	CAV
Maj	Graham, Donald	O 452825	INF
Capt	Littrell, Ralph S.	O 382403	QMC
Capt	Mantler, Marshall J.	O 1293078	INF
Capt	Dennis, William J.	O 1303120	INF
Capt	Carrington, Philip S.	O 425925	INF
1stLt	Stafford, George T. Jr.	O 438709	CAV
1stLt	Townsend, Robert F.	O 1318344	INF
2ndLt	Dietrich, John L.	O 2011242	INF
WOJG	Nier, John E.	W 2119520	NMB

G-3 AIR

LtCol	Murray, Irvin P.	O 305565	AC
Maj	Piper, Joe H.	O 291955	INF
Maj	Page, John W.	O 325634	INF
Capt	Basinger, Virgil D.	O 1286231	INF

AIR LIAISON

LtCol	Goodwin, Homer L.	O 279814	INF
LtCol	Brovos, George J.	O 183018	INF
LtCol	Martin, James G. IV	O 29280	FA
LtCol	Dunning, Chester H.	O 383618	CAV
Maj	Linden, Norman E.	O 362243	CAV
Maj	Walton, John W.	O 232842	INF
Maj	Buckles, Roscoe C.	O 390668	CAV

Maj	Carvey, John C.	O 357374	INF
Maj	Baldwin, Richard M.	O 268172	INF
Maj	Cothran, James C.	O 342661	INF
Maj	Fry, Kenneth L.	O 354246	INF
Maj	Castle, Alexander M.	O 450580	INF
Maj	Corbin, Walter E.	O 450583	INF
Capt	Marsden, Henry H.	O 329983	INF
Capt	Dubey, William	O 1011863	INF
Capt	Chingos, Peter G.	O 286245	INF
Capt	Rush, James B. L.	O 453578	INF
Capt	Converse, Charles D.	O 1167372	FA
Capt	Adams, William R.	O 1167560	FA
Capt	Watson, James W.	O 376546	INF
Capt	Van Horn, Richard	O 1114317	CE

ATTACHED
11TH SPECIAL FORCE DETACHMENT

LtCol	Powell, Robert I.	O 329025	CAV
Maj	Bartlett, Eben B. Jr.	O 366695	FA
Maj	Davis, Gerald W.	O 366979	CAC
Maj	Thomas, Allison K.	O 1284241	INF
1stLt	Babineau, Raymond P.	O 1319366	INF
1stLt	Ripley, William T.	O 1165940	INF
1stLt	Rosett, Francis C.	O 1014505	INF
1stLt	Le Blanc, Robert J.	O 446454	INF
1stLt	L'Hereault, Roger J.	O 1301169	INF
1stLt	Walsh, Rutherford T.	O 1185152	FA
1stLt	Carroll, Rene E.	O 1002771	INF
1stLt	Kelso, Andrew R.	O 1647118	AUS
2ndLt	Niel, Charles	O 1895386	AUS

3d INFORMATION AND HISTORICAL SERVICE

LtCol	Cole, Hugh M.	O 907578	ORD
Maj	Dayton, Dello G.	O 363889	CAC
Capt	Clark, Ledyard B.	O 1995389	AUS
Capt	Dunkerley, William J.	O 1296185	INF
1stLt	Morris, Harry A.	O 1323456	INF
1stLt	Burts, Theron E. Jr.	O 523601	FA

G-4 SECTION

Brig Gen	Muller, Walter J.	O 12225	GSC
Col	Perry, Redding F.	O 9900	GSC
Col	Cooke, Joseph R.	O 100239	TC
Col	Harrison, William H.	O 292346	GSC
LtCol	Hertzler, John V.	O 348346	GSC
LtCol	Weissinger, William T. III	O 21154	FA
LtCol	Stegner, Albert L.	O 240196	GAC
LtCol	Anderson, Charles E, Jr.	O 348456	FA
LtCol	Burroughs, Vernon R.	O 365881	FA
LtCol	Pirkle, Charles G.	O 354475	CAC
LtCol	Hazelett, Charles W.	O 361771	INF
Maj	McKenna, John F.	O 209052	QMC
Maj	Sandoz, Thomas R.	O 293213	QMC
Maj	Walton, Richard E.	O 311774	INF
Maj	Knecht, Charles H.	O 365420	FA
Maj	Buchan, John	O 311022	CAV
Maj	Morris, Donald K.	O 365296	FA
Maj	Shackelford, Virginius R. Jr.	O 453211	INF
Maj	Gilbert, Harry T. Jr.	O 324211	FAV
Maj	Bracewell, Joseph S. Jr.	O 374240	CAV
Maj	Dunlap, Walter H.	O 353142	CAV
Capt	Baldwin, Lewis W. Jr.	O 374058	FA
Capt	Simmon, B. Jr.	O 405842	CE
Capt	Johnson, Joseph C.	O 1292891	INF
Capt	McCann, John K.	O 1574482	QMC
1stLt	Cox, Clarence B. Jr.	O 1949404	TC
1stLt	Ethier, Raymond E.	O 1595496	QMC
CWO	Pense, Jesse B.	W 2119265	NMB
OJG	Tapp, Marion E.	W 2109702	NMB

ATTACHED

Col	Speidel, George S.	O 18406	GSC
LtCol	Weetman, Harold R.	O 300244	CAV
LtCol	Bretzke, Louis E.	O 267000	TC
Maj	Nagel, William E.	O 475372	TC
Maj	Fuquay, James N.	O 110317	INF
Capt	Platson, Kenneth F.	O 1994678	CMP

G-5 SECTION

Col	Campanole, Nicholas W.	O 1777	GSC
Col	Dalferes, Roy L.	O 10279	GSC
LtCol	Hatch, Azel F.	O 1800398	FA
LtCol	Neilson, David J.	O 135938	AUS
LtCol	Hamilton, Paul	O 16455	INF
LtCol	Phelps, Robert K.	O 178811	INF
LtCol	Bacon, Gasper G.	O 282952	AC
LtCol	Pattou, Albert B.	O 116506	ORD
LtCol	Stephenson, William A. F.	O 506836	CMP
LtCol	Goodwin, George E.	O 271865	FA
LtCol	Lindley, Thomas	O 327212	INF
LtCol	Erion, George L.	O 916562	TC
LtCol	McEwan, Oswald B.	O 328192	FA
Maj	Van Wagenen, James H.	O 265568	FA
Maj	Croft, Richard G.	O 900067	AUS
Maj	Swarm, William R.	O 305192	FA
Maj	Borchert, Joseph J.	O 297890	INF
Maj	Peddy, George E. B.	O 497007	AGD
Maj	Bowman, Clair F.	O 245952	CE
Maj	St Claire, William K.	O 171154	AC
Maj	Weaver, Frank M.	O 236358	INF
Maj	Hanrahan, James C.	O 520279	AUS
Maj	Rainwater, Julius H.	O 518064	AUS
Maj	Dutton, William S.	O 534819	AUS
Maj	Williams, Mick G.	O 389531	CAV
Maj	Sewall, Loyall F.	O 479244	CMP
Maj	Coker, Edwin H.	O 920003	SIG C
Maj	Igloe, Max C.	O 274490	MC
Maj	Perera, Lionel C	O 900986	SIG C
Maj	Schafer, Phillip	O 518292	AUS
Capt	Scott, Thomas W.	O 335776	INF
Capt	Denunzio, Vincent L.	O 175395	CE
Capt	Bentley, Garth A.	O 921983	ORD
Capt	Baxter, Garth A.	O 161146	CMP
Capt	Davis, George W.	O 524746	AUS
Capt	Ritchie, George D.	O 531445	AUS
Capt	Engel, Abraham L.	O 534711	AUS
Capt	Blythe, William W.	O 305895	CMP
1stLt	Ogg, Joseph C.	O 512179	SN C

1stLt	Story, Charles H.	O 1004245	AUS
1stLt	Cooper, John S.	O 1798336	CMP
1stLt	Bleshman, Norman	O 581405	AUS
2ndLt	Booth, George H.	O 2026175	AUS

ATTACHED

Maj	Hughes, Merritt Y.	O 531053	AUS
Capt	Posey, Robert K.	O 228681	CE

ADJUTANT GENERAL SECTION

Col	Cummings, Robert E.	O 7512	AGD
LtCol	Anderson, George E.	O 135060	AGD
LtCol	Manly, Lorraine L.	O 300272	AGD
LtCol	Hartman, Robert W.	O 474092	AGD
LtCol	Carlin, Ralph R.	O 315859	AGD
LtCol	Frey, Clarence V.	O 338891	AGD
Maj	Hill, Samuel T.	O 445356	AGD
Maj	Hamlin, John J.	O 1573254	AGD
Maj	Grass, Frank R.	O 1001793	AGD
Maj	Slosson, Richard L. Jr.	O 1001049	AGD
Capt	Bunin, David C.	O 885856	AGD
Capt	Cory, Charles F.	O 1001760	AGD
Capt	Engler, Howard A.	O 2046628	AGD
Capt	Peden, Jowell L.	O 487956	AGD
Capt	Cahill, Thomas F. Jr.	O 1002591	AGD
Capt	Shwiff, Morris	O 1003840	AGD
1stLt	Turner, Jesse L.	O 497429	AGD
1stLt	Evans, James I.	O 479910	AGD
1stLt	Hamilton, Charles C.	O 1001143	AGD
2ndLt	Burns, William T. Jr.	O 2010500	AGD
CWO	Self, Charlie E.	W 2108565	NMB
CWO	Jones, Floyd M.	W 2108638	NMB

ANTI-AIRCRAFT ARTILLERY SECTION

Col	Gallagher, Ferdinand F.	O 4503	CAC
Col	Chamberlin, Frederick R. Jr.	O 10785	CAC
LtCol	Cox, William A.	O 320286	CAC
LtCol	Watkins, Dacy P.	O 268246	CAC
LtCol	Beldon, Morris C.	O 308851	CAC
Maj	Lockwood, Myron D.	O 315056	CAC
Maj	Graham, Harold E.	O 293467	CAC
Maj	Larsen, Lester J.	O 375774	CAC
Maj	Dunn, Gerold C.	O 1042276	CAC
Capt	Townsend, Lee E.	O 379585	CAC
Capt	Robinson, Michel A.G.	O 25523	CAC
1stLt	Wood, Harry F. Jr.	O 1041063	CAC
1stLt	Walsh, Robert R.	O 1052619	CAC
1stLt	Wynn, John G.	O 521271	CAC
CWO	Schrock, Elmer W.	W 2114296	NMB
WOJG	Kidd, John M. Jr.	W 2132833	NMB

ATTACHED

Capt	Gillis, Thomas S	O 465829	CAC
1stLt	Walker, Frederick L. Jr.	O 448865	CAC
1stLt	Lovell, Jack R.	O 515473	CAC

ARTILLERY SECTION

Brig Gen	Williams, Edward T	O 12818	USA
Col	Singer, Richard C.	O 12756	FA
Col	Heitman, Charles L.	O 18059	FA
LtCol	Martin, William J.	O 287196	FA
LtCol	Tilghman, Mayo T.	O 269816	FA
LtCol	Ross, Philip R.	O 245130	FA
Maj	Anderson, Jesse G.	O 366586	FA
Maj	Dunn, Jerry F.	O 397765	FA
Maj	Cross, James F. III	O 350647	FA
Maj	Grier, William A.	O 306867	FA

Maj	Wilson, Bryce	O 364893	FA
Maj	Butts, Mitchell B.	O 1165165	FA
Capt	Mape, Vance C. Jr.	O 423474	FA
Capt	Morse, Charles A. II	O 411574	FA
Capt	Evans, James H. Jr.	O 1165069	FA
Capt	Chamberlin, James C.	O 1165481	FA
Capt	Anderson, Arthur V.	O 1172733	FA
1stLt	Yurkanan, George M.	O 516503	FA
CWO	Brooks, Charles H.	W 2119343	NMB

CHAPLAIN SECTION

Col	O'Neill, James H	O 16370	CH
Maj	Zorn, George L.	O 354487	CH
Maj	Metcalf, George R.	O 484009	CH
Capt	Callanan, John J.	O 439175	CH
Capt	Hagemann, Frank G. Jr.	O 442271	CH
Capt	Hanley, Philip L.	O 526808	CH
Capt	Anderson, Walter R.	O 526889	CH

CHEMICAL WARFARE SERVICE SECTION

Col	Wallington, Edward C.	O 3838	CWS
Maj	Latta, James E.	O 301747	CWS
Capt	Truslow, Frank O.	O 399823	CWS
Capt	Vaughn, John G. Jr.	O 501474	CWS
1stLt	Bolton, Raymond F.	O 1038336	CWS
WOJG	Johnson, Max F.	W 2121091	NMB

ATTACHED

Maj	Munn, James F.	O 395991	CWS

ENGINEER SECTION

Brig Gen	Conklin, John F.	O 3777	CE
Col	Tully, David H.	O 16075	CE
Col	Morris, George A.	O 266651	CE
Col	Starbird, Alfred D.	O 18961	CE
LtCol	Foley, Robert J.	O 299855	CE
LtCol	Smith, C. Cabanne	O 225519	CE
LtCol	Luna, Raymond C.	O 339326	CE
LtCol	Privette, William P.	O 264574	CE
Maj	Anderlitch, Frank	O 271147	CE
Maj	Hogan, William J.	O 316959	CE
Maj	Garlick, James M.	O 342479	CE
Maj	Rodes, Wilmer E.	O 376507	CE
Maj	Lancaster, Lawrence S.	O 409326	CE
Maj	Merzweiler, John M.	O 285489	CE
Maj	Dickson, Fielding B.	O 316513	CE
Capt	Meyer, George S.	O 295082	CE
Capt	McKelvy, Volney L.	O 381243	CE
Capt	Bernard, Edgar L.	O 391727	CE
Capt	Baker, Donald A.	O 296848	CE
Capt	Austin, James W. Jr.	O 284080	CE
Capt	Cahill, William A.	O 1107842	CE
1stLt	Brackbill, Cletus R	O 412595	CE
1stLt	Ireton, Hap W.	O 1106845	CE
1stLt	Silvermann, Arthur	O 1110256	CE
1stLt	Solomekin, Walter J.	O 1112992	CE
1stLt	Collins, Elijah A. Jr.	O 1109211	CE
1stLt	Hartwell, Charles M.	O 520530	CE
1stLt	Kallendorf, Charles E.	O 1114577	CE
2ndLt	Heybeck, Kingston, S.	O 1111120	CE
2ndLt	Benton, Kelly E.	O 2006617	CE
CWO	Hilton, George W. Jr.	W 2114297	NMB

ATTACHED

1681ST Engineer Survey Liaison Team, Type No 1

LtCol	Kennedy, Daniel	O 469535	CE
Maj	Winkelman, Paul F.	O 304140	CE

Maj	Warren, Vernon J.	O 378016	CE
Capt	Bird, Hugh M.	O 453302	CE
1stLt	Niska, Oiva R.	O 1105062	CE

ATTACHED

2890th Engineer Technical Intelligence Team (Research)

Capt	Dennehy, Alexander S.	O 1107903	CE
1stLt	Purtell, John D.	O 1108249	CE
1stLt	Jordan, James C.	O 1550828	CE
2ndLt	Keller, Sidney B.	O 1111161	CE
2ndLt	Schulze, Thomas R.	O 2007875	CE
2ndLt	Winterfelt, Rolf	O 2015728	CE

ATTACHED

Detachment, 652d Engineer Topographic Battalion

1stLt	Van Kamerik, John G.	O 1113497	CE
1stLt	Carney, Edward F.	O 1113133	CE

FINANCE SECTION

Col	Milliken, Charles B.	O 20340	FD
Maj	Rebori, John N.	O 395516	FD
Capt	Zedler, Leonard W.	O1280277	FD
1stLt	Packett, Wilbern L.	O 510523	FD
2ndLt	Skovron, Joseph W.	O 2015684	FD
2ndLt	Bonano, Peter R.	O 2026169	FD

HEADQUARTERS COMMANDANT SECTION

Col	Bratton, Rufus S.	O 3726	INF
Col	Hoag, John A.	O 3251	FA
Col	Kelley, Fred H.	O 174046	INF

LtCol	Baker, Denzil L.	O 307437	INF
Maj	Gooding, Clarence E.	O 20258	INF
Capt	McAlister, James E.	O 386876	INF
Capt	Marsden, Henry H.	O 329983	INF
Capt	Cochran, Raymond P.	O 390500	INF
Capt	Straw, Robert A.	O 1295622	INF
Capt	Bright, Sterrell J.	O 1300592	INF
1stLt	Silverman, Arthur	O 1110256	CE
1stLt	Campbell, Arthur W.	O 1180144	FA
1stLt	Campbell, Robert E.	O 456021	INF
1stLt	Walters, Vernon A.	O 1582243	QMC
WOJG	Zintgraff, Alfred C.	W 2108750	NMB

INSPECTOR GENERAL SECTION

Col	Park, Clarence C	O 7176	IGD
Col	Bower, Ralph E.	O 6610	IGD
LtCol	Curtis, Karl W.	O 183810	IGD
LtCol	Reeves, Lewis A.	O 244583	IGD
LtCol	Duff, Peter D.	O 420540	IGD
LtCol	Nelson, Clarence J.	O 291394	IGD
LtCol	Ronan, Edward I.	O 307986	IGD
Maj	Helm, Floyd H. Jr.	O 328650	IGD
Capt	Muse, Moses P.	O 237167	IGD
Capt	Rodgers, Ben O.	O 283454	IGD
Capt	Erdmann, Charles W.	O 392438	IGD
Capt	Latham, Brice M.	O 348994	IGD
Capt	Sproul, Archibald A.	O 406823	IGD
Capt	Patterson, Arthur V. Jr.	O 347318	IGD
Capt	Duwe, Miles S.	O 367081	IGD
Capt	Thorne, Rodger H.	O 408716	IGD
Capt	Hayes, Julian M.	O 1041163	IGD
Capt	Murray, Lemuel F.	O 363659	IGD
Capt	Cude, Harold E. Jr.	O 367705	IGD
Capt	Sage, Nathaniel M. Jr.	O 409194	IGD
Capt	Church, Edward H.	O 407879	IGD
Capt	Cordes, Erwin H	O 466327	IGD
1stLt	Konopka, Wenceslaus F.	O 1109427	CE
WOJG	Leoni, Eli	W 2119421	NMB

JUDGE ADVOCATE GENERAL SECTION

Col	Cheever, Charles E.	O 14712	JAGD
Col	Joseph, Robert E.	O 301342	JAGD
LtCol	Givens, Raymond	O275830	FA
LtCol	Allen, Gilbert M. Jr.	O16912	INF
LtCol	O'Connell, Edward M.	O 19563	INF
LtCol	Wade, Ralph M.	O 173499	INF
LtCol	Langeluttig, Albert G.	O 171236	INF
Maj	Thomsen, Purroy E.	O 289470	INF
Maj	Moore, Andre B.	O426645	JAGD
Maj	Denson, William D.	O 900415	JAGD
Maj	Smith, Everett E.	O 2051920	JAGD
Capt	Wilson, Kenneth R.	O 278317	INF
Capt	Hofstetter, Fred W.	O 271250	INF
1stLt	Vaughn, Clarence R. Jr.	O 445784	CAV
1stLt	McKay, Dwight	O 1012042	AUS
1stLt	Beitelshees, Richard D.	O 1184351	FA
2ndLt	McMahon, Patrick W.	O 280076	INF
2ndLt	Wright, Morris	O 2001183	AUS
2ndLt	Reid, John J.	O 2015848	AUS
2ndLt	Raelson, Arthur I.	O 2015880	AUS

MEDICAL SECTION

Brig Gen	Hurley, Thomas D.	O 4090	USA
Col	Hartford, Thomas J.	O 18330	
Col	Perkins, Clell B.	O 8678	VC
Col	Weeks, James J.	O 8738	DC
Col	Sperry, James R.	O 9478	VC
Col	Coates, John B. Jr.	O 20924	MC
Col	Odom, Charles B.	O 480718	MC
LtCol	Jones, Thomas B.	O 905675	MC
LtCol	Weil, Nathan Jr.	O 355583	MC
LtCol	Hood, Robert I.	O 360548	MC
LtCol	Dubuy, Carl T.	O 23650	MC
LtCol	Talkington, Perry C.	O 317931	MC

LtCol	Killingsworth, Winfred P.	O 467018	MC
Maj	Agar, Charles C.	O 442415	SN C
Maj	Chartock, Abraham	O 24638	MC
Maj	Lyman, Irving R.	O 24319	MC
Maj	Brown, Sherman W.	O 452434	MAC
Maj	Sinclair, Bernice J.	N 720948	ANC
Maj	Stubbins, William M.	O 369466	MC
Maj	Ingmand, Eugene B.	O 350176	VC
Maj	Hood, George B.	O 426174	MC
Maj	Weitz, Henry A.	O 419889	MC
Maj	Cassidy, John L.	O 1684844	MC
Maj	Cooper, Theodore W.	O 1541730	MAC
Capt	Kastner, Manuel C.	O 304957	VC
Capt	Avery, S. Kingdon	O 23684	DC
Capt	Allen, Frank Jr.	O 357214	DC
Capt	Connors, David A.	O 307065	MC
Capt	McNicholas, James D.	O 1533631	MAC
Capt	Hamilton, William M.	O 1542621	MAC
Capt	Wise, Richard K.	O 1534192	MAC
Capt	Blair, Max K.	O 1544332	MAC
1stLt	Hedlund, Arthur R.	O 1546737	MAC
1stLt	Schumacher, Peter J.	O 1546559	MAC
CWO	Monuszko, Stanley	W 2119516	NMB

ORDNANCE SECTION

Col	Bricker, L. Monroe	O 7245	ORD
Col	Nixon, Thomas H.	O 9326	ORD
Col	O'Grady, Gerald B.	O 164475	ORD
Col	Van Syckle, David L.	O 16425	ORD
Col	Horridge, Joseph	O 17555	ORD
LtCol	De Guire, Merlin L.	O 19446	ORD
LtCol	Kling, Carl V.	O 370791	ORD
LtCol	Daniel, Kenneth R.	O 343224	ORD
LtCol	Pfeiffer, Gilbert L.	O 370776	ORD
Maj	Bessom, Leonard C.	O 420056	ORD
Maj	Rumazza, Carlo R.	O 308842	ORD
Maj	Burke, Hubert D.	O 341064	ORD
Maj	Foltz, Warren D.	O 290854	ORD
Maj	Beidler, John K.	O 321099	ORD

Maj	Frisch, Lawrence V.	O 497047	ORD
Maj	Burch, Sanford B.	O 1573820	ORD
Maj	Sell, Russell B.	O 503239	ORD
Capt	Del Colliano, Gerald V.	O 316444	ORD
Capt	Thompson, Paul V.	O 489923	ORD
Capt	Leitner, Elmer J.	O 1573358	ORD
Capt	Heidenheim, Roger S.	O 912541	ORD
Capt	Miller, Ervin	O 1550455	ORD
Capt	Hansen, Frederick O.	O 1548827	ORD
Capt	Flanigan, William A.	O 1552063	ORD
Capt	Williams, James E.	O 1555788	ORD
1stLt	Cottingham, James C.	O 1555675	ORD
WOJG	Johnston, Purl H.	W 2107944	NMB
WOJG	Perry, Robert E.	W 2121081	NMB

ATTACHED

Capt	Lord, Wilfred J.	O 364916	ORD
1stLt	Englert, Robert L.	O 1551200	ORD

PROVOST MARSHALL SECTION

Col	Clayton, Phillip C.	O 5210	CAV
Col	Engerud, Harold	O 11716	CAV
Col	MacDonald, John C.	O 8402	CAV
LtCol	Edwards, Johnson P.	O 235024	FA
LtCol	Moore, Harley L. Jr.	O 387634	INF
Maj	McDowell, Joseph E.	O 353069	INF
Capt	Thom, Victor L.	O 334635	CAV
Capt	Lewis, Robert D.	O 388475	CMP
Capt	Millard, George B.	O 473123	CWS
Capt	Dannenfeldt, Karl H.	O 1283919	INF
Capt	Gunner, William R.	O 1797993	CMP
1stLt	Emrich, Harold L.	O 1798661	CMP
1stLt	McAuliffe, Eugene V.	O 1320064	INF
1stLt	Oberleitner, Michael E.	O 1798047	CMP
1stLt	O'Connell, William L.	O 1798696	CMP
2ndLt	Hartman, Sidney	O 1030250	CAV

183

2ndLt	Klein, Charles E.	O 2008300	CMP
2ndLt	Norman, Henry J.	O 2015729	AUS
WOJG	Broyles, Edward S.	W 2113919	NMB

13th CID (Attached to Provost Marshal Section)

Capt	Rosengarden, Joseph	O 1798402	CMP

9th CID (Attached to Provost Marshal Section)

1stLt	Gorham, John H.	O 1798348	CMP

PUBLIC RELATIONS SECTION

Col	Guenther, Gustav B.	O 6741	GSC
Col	Blakeney, Charles C.	O 15438	GSC
LtCol	Hunter, Kent A.	O 114009	AUS
LtCol	Quirk, James T.	O 904528	QMC
Maj	Owens, James P.	O 1030280	CAV
Maj	Widmer, Percy, D.	O 508707	INF
Maj	Deane, Ernest C.	O 412496	QMC
Capt	Drake, William A.	O 243164	INF
Capt	Mayo, John B.	O 423686	INF
Capt	Witty, Donald L.	O 2044495	AUS
1stLt	Long, Theodore S.	O 1001393	AGD
2ndLt	Hahn, Erwin W.	O 2009818	AUS

ATTACHED

Capt	Brown, Lester C.	O 1894884	AUS
Capt	Campbell, James W.	O 1010317	CAV
Capt	Straub, Edwin C.	O 1177201	FA
Capt	Durant, Cecil B.	O 1294636	INF
Capt	Prout, Ralph H.	O 560243	AC
Capt	Lamb, Joe B.	O 1314794	INF
1stLt	Nedelman, Julius	O 1173727	FA
1stLt	Darby, Roy E. Jr.	O 1002405	AUS
1stLt	Schleicher, Everett M.	O 1183758	FA
1stLt	Wolever, John F.	O 1307607	INF

1stLt	Exner, Herbert G.	O 1644204	SIG C
1stLt	Manzi, Arthur J.	O 1306441	INF
1stLt	Schutter, Robert E.	O 520762	FA

QUARTERMASTER SECTION

Col	Busch, Everett	O 7260	QMC
Col	Wood, Fenton M.	O 166365	QMC
Col	West, R. John Jr.	O 16925	QMC
Col	Beine, Helmuth E.	O 11910	QMC
LtCol	Bender, James W.	O 297342	QMC
LtCol	Pack, Dallas B.	O 370539	QMC
LtCol	Warner, William A.	O 257460	QMC
LtCol	Lynch, Charles E.	O 340754	QMC
Maj	Gimblin, Bert H.	O 277462	QMC
Maj	Kemmerer, Frank	O 486914	QMC
Maj	Samuels, Howard J.	O 423227	QMC
Maj	Hemerda, Louis Jr.	O 401969	QMC
Maj	Hoy, Charles E.	O 394824	QMC
Maj	Cotter, Edward T.	O 1573133	QMC
Capt	Kane, Leo M.	O 24569	QMC
Capt	Matthews, Emmitt L.	O 1573396	QMC
Capt	Creed, Edward P.	O 911619	QMC
Capt	Smith, Thomas P.	O 453030	QMC
Capt	Bartlett, Anderson G.	O 311168	QMC
Capt	Kiehl, Elmer R.	O 467258	QMC
Capt	Hollister, Robert S.	O 1574447	QMC
Capt	Broughton, William R.	O 1573072	QMC
Capt	Cohen, Harold W.	O 1585288	QMC
Capt	Shaw, Kenneth W.	O 379069	QMC
1stLt	Cozad, William W.	O 24552	QMC
1stLt	Lee, Robert E.	O 1591261	QMC
1stLt	Den Adel, Glenn C.	O 2000172	QMC
2ndLt	Updegraft, Kenneth E.	O 2015722	QMC
CWO	Bugden, George B.	W 2108752	NMB
WOJG	Pinnell, William H.	W 2129369	NMB

SIGNAL SECTION

Col	Hammond, Elton F.	O 12291	SIG C
Col	Pulsifer, Arthur	O 12211	SIG C
Col	Haswell, Claude E.	O 12731	SIG C
LtCol	Brickson, Herbert O.	O 263512	SIG C
LtCol	Dias, Arthur F.	O 204905	SIG C
LtCol	Lowdermilk, Lee O.	O 279353	SIG C
LtCol	Riggs, Homer	O 230222	SIG C
LtCol	Nagle, Gerald F.	O 220660	SIG C
LtCol	Germain, Louis V.	O 398283	SIG C
LtCol	Wood, Walter H. Jr.	O 365766	SIG C
Maj	Flint, Charles W.	O 371887	SIG C
Maj	Kee, J. Martin	O 372948	SIG C
Maj	Higinbotham, Stephen C.	O 452734	SIG C
Maj	Williamson, Willard J.	O 441855	SIG C
Capt	Warren, Edward D.	O 905009	SIG C
Capt	Rus, Albert F.	O 272765	SIG C
Capt	Harral, Philip W.	O 372316	SIG C
Capt	Sprague, Denton E.	O 360211	SIG C
Capt	Devine, Edmund A. Jr.	O 1633157	SIG C
Capt	Schoenenberger, Paul H.	O 516015	SIG C
1stLt	Scott, Clarence E.	O 492665	SIG C
1stLt	Silber, Gene R.	O 1635331	SIG C
1stLt	Buchanan, Ronald E.	O 1639965	SIG C
1stLt	Walker, Julius B.	O 1634440	SIG C
1stLt	Dalton, Orson A.	O 1641117	SIG C
1stLt	Carpenter, Deverton	O 1637158	SIG C
WOJG	Hickman, Rolland H.	W 2109716	NMB

ATTACHED

LtCol	Harmon, David	O 508784	SIG C
Maj	Semple, Wesley A.	O 444432	SIG C
Maj	Shockley, Thomas R.	O 317075	SIG C
Capt	Heiwinklel, Hans W.	O 1633954	SIG C
1stLt	Parsons, Don E.	O 1644650	SIG C
1stLt	Caulfield, Donald B.	O 1640882	SIG C
1stLt	Wilson, Cecil L.	O 1643462	SIG C

SPECIAL SERVICE SECTION

Col	Van Buskirk, Kenneth E.	O 255812	FA
Maj	Browning, Homer F.	O 279252	INF
Capt	Gersten, Alvin	O 39776	INF
Capt	Farrell, Paul V.	O 1175430	FA

TANK DESTOYER SECTION

| Brig Gen | Earnest, Herbert L. | O 7282 | USA |
| Col | Berry, Logan C. | O 15752 | CAV |

(**Note**: These officers served as commanders of the 1st Tank Destroyer Brigade, which served as the Tank Destroyer Section of Third US Army Headquarters. Other commissioned personnel of the Brigade are not listed herein since it is anticipated that the Brigade through regular channels will render a separate report.)

INDEX